PSYCHOLOGY RESEARCH PROGRESS

PSYCHOANALYTIC THEORY

A REVIEW AND DIRECTIONS FOR RESEARCH

PSYCHOLOGY RESEARCH PROGRESS

Additional books in this series can be found on Nova's website under the Series tab.

Additional e-books in this series can be found on Nova's website under the e-book tab.

PSYCHOLOGY RESEARCH PROGRESS

PSYCHOANALYTIC THEORY

A REVIEW AND DIRECTIONS FOR RESEARCH

KEVIN MARTIN

AND

MAXIMILIAN SIEGWARD

EDITORS

nova science publishers
New York

Library of Congress Cataloging-in-Publication Data

ISBN: 978-1-53612-484-2

Published by Nova Science Publishers, Inc. † New York

CONTENTS

PREFACE

This book provides a review on the theory and dynamics of personality organization and development, or psychoanalytic theory. In its first chapter, the findings from "Psychoanalytic Training in Different Settings: The Path (the Experience) and the Outcome" are presented by Gábor Szőnyi M.D., Tímea Kardos, Hanne Stromme, and Svetlozar Vassilev, M.D., PhD, and supported by the European Psychoanalytic Federation (EPF) and the Han Groen-Prakken Psychoanalytic Institute (PIEE). Next, Zoltan Kovary PhD discusses the psychology of artistic creativity and its influence, as well as health in the creative process. Afterwards, Paola Solano and Luca Quagelli look at the latest theoretical perceptions on the link between early traumatic experiences and underrepresented mental areas. Finally, Juhani Ihanus discusses the concept of resistance and its tie to the psychoanalytic setting.

Chapter 1 - The research project "Psychoanalytic Training in Different Settings: The Path (the Experience) and the Outcome", is supported by the European Psychoanalytic Federation (EPF) under the auspices of the Han Groen-Prakken Psychoanalytic Institute (PIEE) and done by an international team (2011 to 2016). This chapter summarizes and discusses major findings from the project.

The task of PIEE was to train analysts and to tutor newly nascent analytic organizations in the countries of the former Soviet Union. Due to lack of local training analysts, the project included and harmonized also cases of shuttle trainings (carried out in another country, in condensed format).

The main purpose of the study was to get a clearer picture whether psychoanalytic education in different training settings resulted in differences in analytic career, competence and practice. Furthermore, the authors explored whether those differences are more within the training experiences and in the mode in which the transformation to becoming an analyst occurs. May the complex interplay of training components equalize the professional outcome?

The subjects of the study were recently graduated analysts (0-7 years post qualification) from all over Europe. For data collection, the authors used semi-structured in-depth interviews (20), and structured questionnaires (on personal analysis experience, supervision, and competence, 71 respondents). The authors developed a special technique to safeguard anonymity and keep confidentiality (of the interviews) in compliance with research ethics. The authors also adopted qualitative analytic methods to their work. Skype interviewing brought new knowledge in that field, e.g., types of fear in the interviewers.

The authors first looked for similarities and differences between those trained under "regular" circumstances and those who were trained under "non-regular" circumstances. Neither the questionnaires' data nor the interviews confirmed a substantial difference between these groups. Therefore, the authors shifted the focus to characteristics of training experiences and professional work.

Regarding motivation to become an analyst the authors found that in the beginning of psychoanalytic training, the desire of "getting healed" and "becoming a professional" are both present. The wish of "getting healed" is stronger and more profound. In addition, a strong component seems to be the participants' longing to be part of the "chosen" ones. The authors also found confluence between primary motivation, personal analyst, supervisors, psychoanalysis, and the analytic community. The authors found that training-analysis satisfaction of the respondents showed no statistical correlation with the self-assessed analytic competence, creativity, or analytic autonomy, but instead, with the degree of feeling connected to the personal analyst.

Another finding of the research was that societal context and organizational culture influence training experience. One third of the interviewees conveyed a strong psychoanalytic identity with strong commitment to the psychoanalytic society. Another third of the interviewees belonged to a group, which had strong identity without good integration into psychoanalytic society. Finally, the last third of the sample showed weak analytic identity and difficulties to integrate into the psychoanalytic community. Most members of the weak analytic identity group belonged to small psychoanalytic societies or study groups.

Chapter 2 - The psychoanalytic approach to creativity and arts has always been one of the most popular and influential utilizations of depth-psychology. The birth of this concept was connected to Freud's very specific and important relationship with the aesthetic phenomena. Apart from the fact that he was an outstanding writer and that in his publications he cited much more writers than scientists, it was not even incidental that he began to investigate the psychology of artistic creativity. His ideas about creativity were based on the theory of sublimation, and studying the creative process he invented an outstanding but much debated research method called psychobiography. During the decades of the 20th century, the psychoanalytic ideas about creativity transformed according to the development of psychoanalytic theory and practice. The most outstanding authors of this research area were ego-psychologist Ernst Kris and British object relations theorists Melanie Klein and Donald Winnicott. In the last decades of the 20th century, different representatives of self-psychology (Heinz Kohut, Daniel Stern, Robert Stolorow & George Atwood) established a new theoretical framework for psychoanalytic creativity research: they broke up with Freud's biologism and concentrated on the importance of personal and intersubjective affective experiences. In this chapter, the author will present these historical-theoretical changes, but the author will focus on two other important topics as well. One of them is the question of illness and health in the creative process, while the other is the influence of psychoanalytic creativity theory on other psychological trends like neo-analytic schools, existential psychology or transpersonal psychology.

Chapter 3 - Freud and Klein maintained that there is no trauma outside the individual's omnipotence. However, Winnicott described the existence of primitive mental functionings stemming from early traumatic impingements that shatter the baby's area of omnipotence that persist throughout adulthood. These areas of primitive mental functioning co-exist, often in a split off and fragmented way, with more mature areas of the personality causing severe impairments in the sense of self and in the capacity of thinking and symbolization. When there is failure in the original encounter with the object the traces of that early trauma cannot be repressed and remain in the mind as registrations of perceptions which, in Freud's words, are formed by raw proto-emotions (such as body-centred sensations, tones, rhythms and postures). Therefore, these traces can emerge during treatment only through non-verbal communicative modes because they have never reached word presentation. Recent contributions on these phenomena suggest that registration of perceptions lie in the mind in negative as 'voids' or 'psychic holes' that - to quote Green - significantly destabilize the mental apparatus. Nowadays, work with borderline and psychotic patients has become more common in psychoanalytic practice and clinicians have to face and deal with unrepresented mental areas seeking transformation and figuration. In this chapter, firstly the authors present some recent theoretical understandings on the origin of unrepresented mental areas and their relationship with early traumatic experiences. Secondly, the authors introduce and discuss some technical issues that foster the development of the first representation of early traumatic experiences within the analytic couple, i.e., the role of the setting; the affective response to the patient's communications in the analyst's bodily countertransference and reverie as well as the role and features of interpretation while working with these patients.

Chapter 4 - The chapter gives first an outline of the concept of resistance in Freudian psychoanalysis. After that, it highlights the vicissitudes of countertransference in psychoanalytic theories from Freudian psychoanalysis to relational, intersubjective and (co-)

constructivist psychoanalytic approaches. The author formulates the concept of “counter-resistance”, as a special form of countertransference, differentiating its intersubjective aspects. This concept is tied to the integrative, relational and reciprocal psychoanalytic setting and process in which both the analysand and the analyst actively work together through unconscious resistance–counter-resistance dynamics to grasp a better understanding about their situation.

In this article, the analysis of counter-resistance is proposed to be the supplementary counterpart of the more traditional analysis of resistance. Different forms and variations of counter-resistance of the analyst are presented. The dynamic interplay between resistance of the analysand and counter-resistance of the analyst can be understood as a mainly unconscious arena where the analysand and the analyst collaborate with, and oppose to, each other, touching upon and enacting the developmental roots of their personal emotions, thoughts, motivations, actions, fantasies, conflicts and creative potential.

Counter-resistance can involve certain basic areas that are explicated to include analytic free association, contact, communication, content/material and change. Individually, resistance and counter-resistance can both hinder change and lead to change. The analyst’s impatience, vulnerability, assertiveness or outright hostility embedded in unconscious counter-resistance positions can have negative effects on the outcome of analysis. The interference between resistance and counter-resistance can sometimes result in co-resistance phenomena, sabotaging change on both sides. However, there may also be successful working through of co-resistance that paves way toward co-constructive mutual insight and transformation.

This chapter is not restricted to the psychoanalytic setting, while the resistance–counter-resistance dynamic interaction applies also to the contexts outside the analytic situation. Thus, the author traces a passage from resistance to counter-resistance, via countertransference, in the psychoanalytic process and in the organization and institutionalization of the psychoanalytic theory and discipline.

In: Psychoanalytic Theory
Editors: K. Martin and M. Siegward

ISBN: 978-1-53612-484-2

Chapter 1

FROM MOTIVATION TO ORGANIZATIONAL INTEGRATION: TRAINING EXPERIENCES OF RECENTLY QUALIFIED PSYCHOANALYSTS[*]

Gábor Szőnyi[1,†], MD, Tímea Kardos[2,#], Hanne Stromme[3,‡] and Svetlozar Vassilev[4,§], MD, PhD

[1]Hungarian Psychoanalytical Society,
Group Analytic Institute Budapest,
and Han Groen-Prakken Psychoanalytic Institute for Eastern Europe
[2]Hungarian Psychoanalytical Society, Hungary

---

[*] The project has received ethical approval by the council of the European Psychoanalytic Federation and is reviewed and registered by the research ethical committee of the Eötvös Lóránd University, Budapest.

[†] Project Leader, Training Analyst (Hungarian Psychoanalytical Society), Training Group Analyst (Group Analytic Institute Budapest), Psychiatrist, Sociologist; Associate Director (Research), Han Groen-Prakken Psychoanalytic Institute for Eastern Europe

[#] Psychoanalyst, Hungarian Psychoanalytical Society, Hungary

[‡] Associate Professor, Clinical Psychology, Department of Psychology, University of Oslo; Psychoanalyst (Norwegian Psychoanalytic Society), Norway

[§] Assistant Professor, New Bulgarian University, Sofia; Training and Supervising Analyst of the Bulgarian Psychoanalytic Society, Bulgaria.

[3] Clinical Psychology, Department of Psychology, University of Oslo, and Norwegian Psychoanalytic Society, Norway
[4]Assistant Professor at New Bulgarian University, Sofia and Training and Supervising Analyst of the Bulgarian Psychoanalytic Society, Bulgaria

ABSTRACT

The research project "Psychoanalytic Training in Different Settings: The Path (the Experience) and the Outcome", is supported by the European Psychoanalytic Federation (EPF) under the auspices of the Han Groen-Prakken Psychoanalytic Institute (PIEE) and done by an international team (2011 to 2016). This chapter summarizes and discusses major findings from the project.

The task of PIEE was to train analysts and to tutor newly nascent analytic organizations in the countries of the former Soviet Union. Due to lack of local training analysts, the project included and harmonized also cases of shuttle trainings (carried out in another country, in condensed format).

The main purpose of the study was to get a clearer picture whether psychoanalytic education in different training settings resulted in differences in analytic career, competence and practice. Furthermore, we explored whether those differences are more within the training experiences and in the mode in which the transformation to becoming an analyst occurs. May the complex interplay of training components equalize the professional outcome?

The subjects of the study were recently graduated analysts (0-7 years post qualification) from all over Europe. For data collection, we used semi-structured in-depth interviews (20), and structured questionnaires (on personal analysis experience, supervision, and competence, 71 respondents). We developed a special technique to safeguard anonymity and keep confidentiality (of the interviews) in compliance with research ethics. We also adopted qualitative analytic methods to our work. Skype interviewing brought new knowledge in that field, e.g., types of fear in the interviewers.

We first looked for similarities and differences between those trained under "regular" circumstances and those who were trained under "non-regular" circumstances. Neither the questionnaires' data nor the interviews confirmed a substantial difference between these groups. Therefore, we shifted the focus to characteristics of training experiences and professional work.

Regarding motivation to become an analyst we found that in the beginning of psychoanalytic training, the desire of "getting healed" and "becoming a professional" are both present. The wish of "getting healed" is stronger and more profound. In addition, a strong component seems to be the participants' longing to be part of the "chosen" ones. We also found confluence between primary motivation, personal analyst, supervisors, psychoanalysis, and the analytic community. We found that training-analysis satisfaction of the respondents showed no statistical correlation with the self-assessed analytic competence, creativity, or analytic autonomy, but instead, with the degree of feeling connected to the personal analyst.

Another finding of the research was that societal context and organizational culture influence training experience. One third of the interviewees conveyed a strong psychoanalytic identity with strong commitment to the psychoanalytic society. Another third of the interviewees belonged to a group, which had strong identity without good integration into psychoanalytic society. Finally, the last third of the sample showed weak analytic identity and difficulties to integrate into the psychoanalytic community. Most members of the weak analytic identity group belonged to small psychoanalytic societies or study groups.

Keywords: psychoanalysis, psychoanalytic training experiences, training motivation, personal analyst, Skype interviewing, analytic organizations, supervision

I. Introduction – The Birth of the Study

Training is a core issue in psychoanalysis, for the International Psychoanalytical Association (IPA) and for its national (composing) organizations. The personal analysis part makes analytic training "non-regular" for academic education; this has prevented the integration of clinical psychoanalysis into the university system. Notwithstanding, most psychotherapy training models the analytic educational structure.

The Beginning of Psychoanalytic Training in Eastern Europe and the PIEE

Before the Second World War and during the Soviet occupation (influence) that followed, there were no organized analytic groups in any of the so called Eastern-European countries (except for Hungary). Yet, in almost all of the countries there were individuals who were not only interested in psychoanalysis but found ways to get training, as well. A few of these people also achieved formal (direct) membership in the IPA prior to World War 2. Those persons usually had a few people who became interested in the field and obtained some training from them. However, those groups never reached the critical mass to form an analytic organization. Furthermore, the political circumstances did not tolerate the foundation of such organizations, either.

Such activities bear similarities to the birth of analytic organizations in many pre-WW2 Western European countries (e.g., in Scandinavia), but the development was destroyed under the Soviet occupation.

Several Western European societies were destroyed due to World War 2 and Nazi regimes. In many countries, there was a period of "underground" psychoanalysis (e.g., in the occupied countries – France, the Netherlands). There are some components of the re-organizational period of Western European analytic societies that can be observed in the development of Eastern European analytic organizations after the fall of the Soviet Union. These are help of training from stronger societies, shuttle type components in training of new analysts, travelling training analysts; period of underground training; outstanding figures who commit themselves to the preservation of psychoanalysis in the country and the task to cope with problems inherited from totalitarian regimes. A major motif to organize international meetings and, later, to establish the European Psychoanalytic Federation (EPF) was to help the development and (re)-integration of the reviving societies (Groen-Prakken, 2016).

During the eighties, the last decade before the fall of the Soviet empire, the interest in psychoanalysis along with the number of individual connections increased in the above mentioned Eastern European countries.

In addition to that, there were a growing number of active, committed analysts eager to help in spreading the analytic movement. On the organizational level, Eastern European committees were established both within the IPA and the EPF.

Hungary: in Budapest, founded by Ferenczi in 1913, the psychoanalytic movement was part of the first wave of the establishment of analytic societies. It also played an important role in the development of international psychoanalysis. After the Communist takeover in 1948, the Hungarian Society was forced to dissolve. However, the personal continuation of training (and direct IPA membership of a number of Hungarian analysts) was maintained, and a formal organizational re-integration started in 1975. This ended in 1989.

After the fall of the Soviet Union, the social-political changes in Eastern Europe opened huge white territory for IPA organized psychoanalysis. Demand on training and urge to promote development reached an unimagined amount of cross-border activity between individuals, as well as analytic organizations. Boundary conditions enforced/invited training settings which differed from regular training in established institutes.

These new settings included:

- analysts who went for analytic training to other countries (first to France, Germany, and England) and later returned home;
- analysts who immigrated earlier, were trained in the new country, and returned for shorter time or repatriated;
- analysts who received training from the few old ones locally;
- analysts who received shuttle training (see later);
- analysts who received a "condensed" type of training.

All the above initiatives were supported by individuals and analytic societies. Thus some negative side effects also surfaced, such as the preservation of helper-helped relationships.

In 2002, the IPA and the EPF jointly founded the Han Groen-Prakken Psychoanalytic Institute for Eastern Europe (PIEE). To further enhance foundation of study groups in those countries, the task was to integrate, organize, and harmonize the individual initiatives.

The PIEE was an organizational experiment. Being independent from local analytic organizations, the PIEE had no earlier models. It was a provisional organization with an international board. Personal analysis and supervision was carried out by training analysts from the different national societies. The PIEE represented the first joint venture in training between the IPA and a regional organization (EPF). Experience acquired by the PIEE helped to establish a sister organization called Instituto Latinoamericano de Psicoanalisis (ILAP), and to organize the China training project. The PIEE ended its mission in 2014.

By 2016, there were new societies or study groups established in Bulgaria, Croatia, Romania, Moscow (2), Poland, Serbia, Czech Republic, and Ukraine. Furthermore, there are new organizations in the process of being founded in Belorussia, South Russia, and St. Petersburg.

Questions of Analytic Training

Debate on training is a frequent topic. It is difficult to find any aspect or dimension which has not been raised again and again critically, except for the dumb first 25 years after the introduction of international requirements (Balint 1948). This must be rooted in the training, which is mirrored in the question: making or becoming an analyst. Innumerable papers, studies and committees have been dedicated to explore those peculiarities.

The project “Psychoanalytic training in different settings: the path (the experience) and the outcome” has ties back to the Committee on Psychoanalytic Education (IPA-COMPSED) and personal continuation from the EPF’s Working Party on Education (WPE).

IPA-COMPSED, which worked in the nineties made a research proposal to the IPA, at the end of its work. In their research proposal they focused “on the different aspects and components of training, such as the selection and selection criteria of training analysts; the parallel run of training analysis and supervision; formal criteria of training analysis; procedures of the evaluation process; participation of candidates in society life; the extent of theoretical pluralism; and, last but not least: "Who are the leaders or what are the models of the institute – clinicians, theorists, administrators, child or adult analysts, supervisors, or training analysts?"

They made the following hypotheses:

- "Candidates trained in a particular model of psychoanalytic education will have more similarities to one another than candidates trained in other psychoanalytic educational models."
- "Individual differences among candidates (in terms of character, background, talent, etc.) will have a greater impact on what kind of analyst they become than the specific model of training."[1]

However, the plan did not develop into a research project.

The EPF Working Party on Education was a 10-year project undertaken from 2000 to 2009 (Erlich-Ginor et al. 2010). The WPE had a multilevel research scheme of interrelated projects.

The idea was to explore different aspects of the training systems, and identify elements that are helpful or would hinder the transmission of psychoanalysis, such as:

Project 1: Who does what – mapping of factual aspects of training

Project 2: Education in Europe, the spectrum of views on psychoanalytic training (Erlich-Ginor et al. 2007)

Project 3: Becoming and being training analyst

Project 4: End of training – evaluation

Project 5: Psychoanalytic competencies

Project 6: Ending process of personal analysis.

Each project tackled a different issue and used a different methodology, appropriate to the research question. Among others, they

[1] Corrected proposal by COMPSED, p. 1; IPA internal material.

found that senior analysts are quite good at recognizing a competent analyst (we "know it when we see it"), but we are much less able to describe the path to this transformation. There seems to be a need for small-group activities to facilitate the complex task of integrating theory, clinical experience, as well as emotional and intellectual development.

In connection with the WPE work, Tuckett (2005) raised the question: "How can we objectify and do justice to our global subjective judgment of a candidate's competence?" From the experience gained from group-work in a structured meeting of training analysts, he proposed three parameters (the participant observational frame; the conceptual frame; and the interventional frame), which can be used for competency assessment (Junkers, Tuckett, Zachrisson 2008). The complex method is under further development in the End of Training Evaluation Project (ETEP) (Eike 2016).

Experiences of PIEE and the Urge to Study Different Training Experiences

Understandably, intense interest, characterized by enthusiasm and deep doubts, encompassed the Eastern European development of psychoanalysis. The critical considerations could be summarized in the question: Would the PIEE produce, due to those exceptional training circumstances, "second-class" analysts? The reservations called for research. However, the first 10 years of the PIEE indicate that PIEE trainees are on the same level at qualification as the candidates of established European societies. Qualification assessments were always done with participation of external training analysts.

Because of lack of local training analysts, a large part of the training analysis was carried out in shuttle format (Bollas & Diatkine 2010). If there was no *supervision* possibility in loco – which remains often the case even when personal analysis can be provided by local (interim) training analysts – then there was a combination of regular once-a-week face-to-face and skype (earlier e-mail, fax, or phone) sessions. If the supervisor lived in the same place where the shuttle analytic sessions were held, then additional face-to-face supervision meetings were scheduled. Supervision had to run parallel with the analysis done by the candidate.

Theoretical training (seminars) were provided in most cases (also) in blocks, – the "Amsterdam" seminars, the same curriculum in Russian (TSR), and the PIEE schools.

We define the different settings as follows:

Shuttle (training analysis) format includes

- visiting periods usually of 2-6 weeks together;
- 3-6 in a year;
- during the visiting period, the sessions are held in a condensed way (more than one session a day);
- during the visiting period, the candidate lives in the city of the analyst;
- the visit periods are usually agreed from case to case;
- the visits may differ in duration and session numbers;
- Skype sessions may be held during the long breaks but do not count in the PIEE model.

From case to case, the shuttle contracts are individually adjusted.

Condensed training (analysis) means that

- the sessions are compiled to be held together over a few days (more than one session per day) instead of spreading them out over a period of time (3-5 in a week, depending on the model);
- the candidate leaves home at least for one night;
- the process goes on in a regularly repetitive way, e.g., the same 2 days in the week or condensed sessions every second week (like the training of Estonians in Helsinki);
- shorter distance and good travel connections make the regularity possible.

According to personal feedback, the condensed structure can make separation problems more difficult than regular or shuttle training.

Regular format means that

- the sessions are distributed over different days;
- without condensation;
- have fixed time schedule;
- little distance and good travel connections make that frame possible – candidate and analyst live in the same city or within a reasonable distance.

An important aspect is that the candidates move between different cultures and countries as part of the training. Szőnyi and Stájner-Popovič (2008) summarized the connections of formal variations of training. They called attention to the fact that shuttle analysis/training also means shuttle life for the candidates.

The Project and Its Team

In 2010 and 2011, several interrelated circumstances allowed us to begin the present study. At that time, initial questions within the PIEE were emphasized differently. Instead of trying to evaluate possible differences between "regular" and "non-regular" training – without having a standard picture of what a good-enough post-qualification analyst would look like –, we turned our attention to the paths and experiences during the training process. We opened the project to all analysts in Europe who had qualified 0-7 years before the study started. We chose the time-span of being a "novice analyst."

The study was run by an international team[2], with financial support and control by the EPF, under the auspices of the PIEE. The composition of the team mirrored the dynamics of a group comprising clinicians and researchers (see the thematic issue of Psychotherapy Research 2015). The team developed the design of the projcct, and adjusted details along the data-collection and data-analysis period. A smaller part of the group is now in the process of compiling the work to publish the results.

Whilst, with one exception, all team members were analyst-clinicians, some of us have also worked at universities and had experience in empirical research. Others prioritize more an analytic understanding, which helped the group remain critical in both directions.

The project – with a pilot study character – covers a broad range of topics, concerning the experiences during and after analytic training.

We expected to gain more clarity on psychoanalytic education in different training settings. Setting here refers both to the form of training (regular and shuttle), and to the institutional environment (established-traditional institutes exceptionally structured and pioneer phase ones). We contemplated whether the various training settings prompted differences in the sense of analytic competence and practice (analytic career); or whether those differences could be found more within the training experiences and in the way in which the transformation to becoming an analyst takes place or occurs. This might be of high importance for all involved in analytic-education matters. We chose the novice-analyst phase, as we assumed that the relatively fresh training experience promoted the ability of these newly graduated analysts to remember more details.

We hoped to get a clearer picture whether the investments (of trainees, trainers and institutions-organizations) are appropriate, higher or lower than what the "production" of analysts would require.

---

[2] Members of the team for longer or shorter: Bien Filet (Netherlands), Mira Erlich-Ginor (Israel), Ursula von Goldacker (Germany), †Arkadijs Pancs (Latvia), Tatyana Pushkarova (Ukraine), Hanne Stromme (Norway), Tímea Kardos (Hungary), Leena Klockars (Finland), Joan Schachter (Great Britain), Gábor Szőnyi (Hungary), Ioana Terzieva (Bulgaria), Toma Tomov (Bulgaria), Sverre Varvin (Norway), Svetlozar Vassilev (Bulgaria).

We also expected to find out more about how analytic training is converted into professional practice in our times and what the learnt competencies are used for. From the above we sought to understand more why it is worth to start analytic training.

Additionally, we aimed to learn more about the experience of regular training, which can be compared with other new training experiments in the future.

The first findings indicated that differences were formed more by factors other than the type of the training setting. Consequently, we shifted our focus to characteristics of training experiences and professional work.

II. Method

Project Settings

The project was built on questionnaires and interviews. By mediation of the European psychoanalytic societies we invited analysts, who had received their qualification within 7 years of the start of the project, to participate. Originally, we planned to interview both members of the training analytic respectively the supervisory pairs (training analyst – candidate; supervisor – candidate). However, we decided not to pursue this plan, as it would have worked against our targeted level of anonymity.

Those who signed up were provided detailed explanation about the project. They received a 4-digit code to complete the online questionnaires, and also to register for an interview when appropriate. The recruiting period lasted from fall 2011 to the end of 2012. We finished the data gathering from the questionnaires at the end of 2013, and the interviews in the summer of 2014.

Altogether we had 71 respondents, and we interviewed 20 analysts of this group. The interviewees were chosen randomly. We developed a system to secure both anonymity and confidentiality (see later). For the interviews we had the planned number of cases (20 + test interviews), but we overestimated the number of possible respondents to the questionnaires

(47-71, varying on the different questionnaires). This forced us to be very careful when forming subgroups and interpreting the quantitative data.

We have not been able to determine the response rate in the questionnaire part of the study. The reason for this is that according to our knowledge the IPA does not collect/summarize the number of graduates/year (although individual societies keep track of the number of own graduates). In addition, it was beyond the possibilities and interest of the current pilot study to try to include the whole population of new graduates all over Europe, or to try to make a representative sample regarding gender and country.

Based on an estimate of the total target population there are 200-300 recently graduated analysts (in Europe. The total number of relevant psychoanalysts in shuttle training in the studied time span was probably below 40 or even 30. In conclusion, the final response rate was not too high. Interestingly, the response rate appeared to be approximately the same for psychoanalysts trained in regular and non-regular settings.

The way psychoanalysts relate to empirical research is an issue on its own. Some potential participants explained to us that they doubted that empirical research based on the subjective reports of the participants would sufficiently explore the complex process of psychoanalytic training. Yet, one may wonder if there is resistance to being exposed to a research group regarding a deeply personal experience such as commitment to psychoanalytic training.

Questionnaires and Interviews

The participants could choose between English and a Russian version of the questionnaires; the vast majority used the English version. The interviews were conducted via Skype; we developed our own methodology for Skype interviewing, which might bring some clarity to the use of Skype in therapeutic settings as well (see later). The questionnaires contained closed questions and were analyzed statistically, whilst the semi structured, in-depth interviews were processed with qualitative methods.

a) The Questionnaires and Scales

We selected four types of questionnaires for the project:

- Formal data questionnaire (developed for the project);
- Psychoanalyst feedback questionnaire (Bush & William 2011);
- Experiences in supervision ('Columbia questionnaire', Cabaniss, Glick & Roose 2001);
- Analytic competencies self-assessment (Filet & Szőnyi, 2009).

Completion of the questionnaires took respondents 60-90 minutes. Retrospectively, we think that for some of the respondents we lost, the required completion time was too long.

Formal Data Questionnaire

In the *"formal data"* questionnaires, we collected information on the setting and duration of personal analysis and supervisions, as well as on the respondent's analytic and analytic psychotherapy practice. For the sake of anonymity, we decided not to ask about the individuals' country/society background or to collect any other personal data. This is because the psychoanalytic community is quite small, even internationally, and only a few people qualify in a society each year. The data gained in these questionnaires served subgroup formation. Therefore, we could omit similar questions from the other questionnaires, thus avoiding repetition.

Psychoanalyst Feedback Questionnaire

To approach the experience of the personal analysis component of the training with a quantitative tool as well, we used a somewhat shortened version of the *psychoanalyst feedback questionnaire*[3]. We kept only the closed questions part which consisted of two major sections: a) outcome (with subsections addressing the 'fit' with the personal analyst, the relation process and the improvement through the process), and b) analyst attribute

[3] A copy of the questionnaire can be obtained by emailing Marshall Bush at <drmbush@pacbell.net>.

(with subsections on the analyst's technique and on the feelings of the respondent about the analysis and the personal analyst). The two sections together comprised 150 Likert type questions. We added a third section (worked out by team member Tatyana Pushkareva), which analyzed the circumstances and special aspects of training more common in shuttle analysis (training).

Columbia Questionnaire

The *Columbia questionnaire on supervision* also targets the *experience* of supervision during analytic training. Therefore it fits our main objective appropriately. It contains 69 Likert questions in twelve subsections, which explore the general subjective assessment of supervision, the supervisory relationship, and how the respondent saw the supervisor's theoretical and technical attitude. There are questions on good and bad experiences, and questions investigating whether the respondent pondered to change supervisor.

Analytic Competencies Self-Assessment

We (Filet and Szőnyi) created the *questionnaire on analytic competences* in the Working Party on Education (WPE, mentioned earlier). It consists of 27 Likert questions and reveals how the importance and specificity of different competencies changed during the transition from being a psychotherapist through candidacy to becoming an analyst. (A major finding from these questionnaires was that psychotherapists believed theoretical knowledge to be more specific/important, while analysts deemed emotional capacities more central. The opinion of candidates took position between the former two groups). In the present project we applied the self-assessing version of the competence questionnaire.

For the statistical analysis we used the scales of the original questionnaires, as well as having developed a couple of our own scales. All scales were checked for reliability, and, in some cases we also reviewed their items. We found all scales highly reliable (Cronbach α above 0.8), expect for the scale titled "separation", which we therefore skipped. We decided that separation should be approached through the interviews.

List of accepted scales in alphabetical order:

1) Acumen to shared unconsciousness; being and acting in it
2) Analytic autonomy and receptive attitude
3) Attachment to - depending on training analyst
4) Classical technique scale
5) Competency level – analytic strength
6) Creativity
7) Emotional resonance, receptiveness and containing
8) Helpful insight scale
9) Negative alliance scale
10) Openness in supervision
11) Positive alliance scale
12) Positive personality qualities scale
13) Positive relational qualities scale
14) Strategic analytic knowledge
15) Supervision satisfaction
16) Supportive technique scale
17) Training analysis satisfaction

In general, we raised two types of questions:

a) Do we find any statistically significant difference between the group of "non-regulars" or shuttlers and the group of "regulars"?
b) Do we find any statistical correlation between the different scales for the whole sample or its meaningful subgroups?[4]

We have used this data primarily as a supplement to the analysis of the interview data.

[4] We owe special thanks to László Bernáth from Eötvös Lóránd University (Budapest) for the statistical analysis of our data.

b) The Interviews

We intended to use the interview findings for more in-depth analysis and to explore aspects of the training that the questionnaires did not cover. The aim of the interviews was to allow participants to tell about their training as they individually experienced it. The number of interviews was chosen in accordance with the purpose of the study (Kvale, 1998). In this case, we planned to conduct twenty interviews.

All interviewees accepted our invitation. By then, they had already gone through a long process of completing extensive questionnaires, indicating a strong attachment to the project, and to their own training. Filling-in these questionnaires also made them feel prepared for the Skype interview, as several of them mentioned. The interview period ended in August 2013.

In the planning phase, the research group decided to focus on the following topics concerning the experiences before, during, and after analytic training:

- Motivations to become a psychoanalyst;
- Experiences of the training analysis;
- Changes during analytic training;
- Experience of separation; regressive periods;
- Training influence on interviewee's life;
- Ending of the analysis; ending training;
- Relationship with the analyst and the supervisors;
- Professional strengths and weaknesses;
- Integration into and role expectation in the analytic society;
- Image about the other training setting, non-regular or regular.

The interviews via Skype consisted of two parts performed on different occasions, namely a preparatory meeting followed by an interview encounter over the next days. The interviews, with a time limit of 90 minutes, were semi-structured with an interview guide developed for the purpose[5]. The guide centred around the nine focal points mentioned above. The interviewers wrote a reflection note after each interview to accommodate relevant aspects of the interview not covered by the transcription. These aspects, for instance are themes that appeared particularly significant to the interviewee.

The interviews were conducted in English, a second language for participants and interviewers alike. Hence one may question the impact on the quality of the data material. Undoubtedly, subtle nuances are lost. On the other hand, the interviewees give the impression that they tried their best to convey relevant emotional training experiences and reflections about their training process. This is probably a reflection of their investment in the research topic. Moreover, due to their extensive education, compared to many other research participants, we consider them particularly able to verbalize their experiences. To some degree, these aspects of our participants counteract the language barrier.

Four interviewers performed the interviews: Three from Eastern and one from Western Europe, three psychologists and one physician. To prepare themselves for the task, the interviewers conducted test interviews among themselves.

To ensure the anonymity of the participants, several procedures were performed. Our project administrator was the only one familiar with the identity of all project participants who were only identified by codes in the data material. Before each interview, the secretary contacted the selected participant to invite him or her to participate in the interview part of the study and acted as a point of contact to receive confirmations of attendance. Additionally, she ensured that the interviewee did not know the interviewer beforehand. Subsequently, she sent the interviewee's email address to the interviewer, thus disclosing them the participant's identity at this time.

---

[5] The interview was done in accordance to the guidelines developed by the research team after an extensive literature search and series of discussions. You can see the guidelines in appendix 2.

Once finished, the audio-taped interviews were sent encrypted with a password[6] to the administrator who forwarded them to one of the two transcribers in the project. Both transcribers signed a confidentiality agreement in advance. All personal and geographical names were left out of the transcription, as well as other potential identification elements. Next, the interviewer assessed the accuracy of the transcription by listening to the interview while simultaneously reading the transcription. In addition, the interviewer also omitted potential identifying remarks in the transcription. Neither the transcriber nor the researchers that later analyzed the interview data knew the identity of the interview pair.

The data material is kept in a central server to which only the members of the research team have access. The team members have access codes, given and known only by the project administrator, and unknown to each other.

c) An Excursus: Experiences with Working out Skype Interviewing

In this project, we have used the online Skype-program to perform the interviews. This new technology in research instigates at least two methodological and one ethical question:

1) What kind of interview alliance is developed on Skype?
2) What kind of data do we receive interviewing on Skype?
3) What kind of ethical challenges are we confronted with when interviewing on Skype?

"Searching within PsycINFO, Web of Science and PubMed, there are only a few articles discussing online-interviewing in social sciences (i.e., Seitz, 2016; Deakin & Wakefield, 2014; Janghorban et al., 2014; Sullivan, 2012), and a couple of newly arrived dissertations within psychotherapy

[6] Audio-taped files were sent to the project secretary via Internet. Three of the interviewers used the freely available programme "Transfer Big Files." One interviewer used "CloudStor," which was the programme used for the purpose at the University of Oslo at that time, along with the encryption programme "7-Zip."

research conduct interviews online (i.e., Ortega, 2017) but not any within psychotherapy training and therapist development."

There are only a few articles discussing online-interviewing in social sciences (i.e., Deakin & Wakefield, 2014; Janghorban et al., 2014; Sullivan, 2012), and none within psychotherapy research, psychotherapy training, or therapist development. This technology has not been used in research within the field of psychoanalysis, although it has been implemented as a supplement in psychoanalytic treatment and supervision.

Qualities of the Interview Relationship

Qualitative research of psychoanalytic training puts its participants in contact with satisfactory experiences as well as painful personal traumata and shortcomings of the training itself. It is not a surprise that it may evoke deep-seated anxieties in both researchers and participants. In-depth interviews allow hidden fears, prejudices, and impasses to be expressed and explored.

The interviewer group already shared some fears before the interview period started:

- Would they be able to develop trustful relationship with the interviewees on Skype?
- Would they be able to provide appropriate data required for the study, not the least taking into consideration the language barrier?
- Is the anonymity of the participants sufficiently ensured when using an online-video program to carry out the interview?

To start with the interview relationship, how did the interviewees experience the interview situation and the interview relationship? At the end of the interviews, the interviewer asked the interviewee about this. Most of the interviewees gave positive feedback. The conversation had evoked memories that for a long time had remained in the silent background. Several said it directly or conveyed it nonverbally that during the interview they had gained new perspective on their training.

Below is an example of an answer we received:

P: It was very nice for me, I think. Not embarrassing or something like that. It was nice to think about analysis, about education again. Nothing comes to my mind, what to add. Maybe to add something about what is good about all this education… [the interviewee further elaborates on her training experience] … So, our conversation was also for me very… I like it. We're talking about a topic that you like, that I like. Isn't it nice? OK?

The participant quoted above doubtlessly had a positive experience of the interview and of the interviewer. Here is another example of the same, focusing on the personal exposure in the interview:

P: It was a bit sad, because I remembered many people who are already not here.

R: Perhaps it was a bit different from what you expected?

P: Uh. No, I didn't expect something specific. I thought we would talk about the training process, perhaps what was, uh, mainly what was a bit different was that it got so personal in a way but, no other way right now.

R: Ok. Mm. I see. Mm. Uh, perhaps you felt that it has been too personal?

P: Uh, personal enough I think. (smiles)

Only a few openly revealed reluctance regarding participation in the interview and only one openly expressed skepticism towards being interviewed. This was related to the interview being recorded:

P: I didn't find anywhere a mention about the recording. It was a very unpleasant surprise for me. And you said that everything will be recorded.

R: Yes. And what is your question about this record?

P: I don't like it.

R: You don't like it?

P: Yes, I don't like it.

The interviewer then explained the anonymity procedure, while simultaneously underlining the freedom of the interviewee to withdraw. The interviewee decided to stay within the study.

However, the quotations above also indicate the troubles with subjective reports. We cannot know if interviewees expressing an exclusively positive attitude hid some fears or objections. We may of course, have some ideas about why some interviewees turned the focus onto the interviewer's experience of the interview. It could have been overwhelming to give feedback by talking directly to the interviewer about him or her, or it could indicate a negative attitude, which the interviewees did not want to convey. The participant focusing on the confidentiality risk of recording the interview conveyed the feeling of being trapped caused by an obligation to a colleague with authority. However, this response may in fact masks other objections not being expressed.

Furthermore, we do not know what second thoughts our interviewees may have had. We invited them to contact us again if they had some questions or comments but no one has utilised their opportunity to do so.

Although they did not mention it in the end, without a doubt, the interviewees also conveyed fears of being interviewed – a parallel to the initial fear of us interviewers. Here is a list of the worries that appeared most frequently:

- "Is my training sufficient and comparable to that of others?"
- "Would my anonymity be ensured?"
- "Would my personal trauma, and, additionally for Eastern Europeans the pitfalls of the training in my country, be understood and respected?"

It is interesting to notice that these fears are found in participants trained in *both* regular and non-regular training.

Data Quality from Skype Interviewing

The most obvious advantage of the Skype interviewing is the possibility to reach potential participants who are unable to do face-to-face interviews due to travel expenses. This factor potentially contributes to the expansion of the sample size, as well as to the diversity of the participants. In this respect, the sample in Skype interviewing to a higher degree can reflect a population. This may lead to an improvement in data validity. On the other hand, restrictions in the conversation on Skype may reduce the quality of the data we receive.

In order to expose the content and the verbal style of the raw data, we present some examples.

About motivation to start training (the participant talks as if it is before the training starts):

> "I don't know how to talk to people, and I don't know nothing about people, I don't know nothing about (laughs) about persons and about, you know, men, women, child, children. So my expectation, yes, I wanted somebody to teach me how to talk with people, with close people, how to understand, what do they tell me, what do they expect from me, can I reach them, can I give them what they expect, uh, like this. Yes, as if to, to, to teach me to, to talk."

About the relationship to the personal analyst:

> "Very bad memory, very bad relationship with my analyst. I didn't like this woman, because of her person, of her personality. But she was holding the setting and being a good analyst. So it worked. But I didn't have any, uh, uh, affinity (…) And I had a negative transfer most of the time (laughs) (…) she spoke very, very few. It was the fashion at this time. The analysts were not speaking. (…) I just remember the systematical interpretations of my analyst. That was really bothering me. I mean she was systematically interpreting, interpreting the separations of vacations, uh. (…) I think she had a lot of trouble with me, and she—I am sure she was speaking of me with her husband, who is also an analyst, because she was very much in trouble with my negative transference."

An experience related to changes in the personal analysis:

> "I didn't know whether what I experienced was a dream or memory—but it was an image of myself as a very small baby and somebody coming to me and going away and playing with me and laughing (…) I knew that I would never be really unhappy again."

An experience from being in shuttle training:

> "Sometimes I wake up in the train at night and ask myself: "Where I am?" And I answer to myself: "I am in the train." And the second question was: "Where are you going to?" [Laughs] If the answer was: "To **C** [shuttle town]" "Oh, it's **C**, it's alright!" But if the answer was: "To home." It was very sad. It was again adaptation, again a lot of problems and so."

Relationship to the leadership of the psychoanalytic society:

> "I don't like the style of leadership in my society, because it's: "If you stay with me, you speak at my congress, if you don't stay with me, you away." It's terrible. (…) An analyst I think, I, today think, yet, uh, narcissistic analyst is not too good analyst, not a good person. (…) I am—I think that our work is continual erosion narcissistic, because we have to leave a space free for another person, and if we are full of our self, you cannot hear another person or love him. (…) It was de-illusion, it was a very de-illusion for me to see that my colleagues are so narcissistic, full of narcissism."

Ethical Challenges When Interviewing via Skype

Simultaneously, another significant question introduced itself to us in the research group: What are the ethical implications of interviewing online? Regarding data material, the interviewer has a fear about surveillance. As an ethical challenge to the interviews, the fear that someone else would get access to the data was a major concern of the research group. As Sullivan (2012) puts forth, when we push the accept button for installing Skype on our PC, we accept - as written in the "small text" - the right of the Skype administration to record our conversations.

Furthermore, it may potentially be possible for hackers now or later to track conversations, locations, and identities of these recordings.

Here is the quotation from the aforementioned incidence. The interviewee is from Eastern Europe:

> R: You said that your supervisors and perhaps also you training analyst were a part of another generation and you haven't talked about the political system; how that contributed to the psychoanalytical society in **A** – the change from a political dictatorship to a democracy?
>
> P: Oh, I don't know. It was a long time ago, this change.
>
> R: So you don't think it had any influence on your process?
>
> [Two breaks in the Skype connection follow where the interview pair only talked about the connection quality. There had not been any break prior to these situations.]
>
> R: Did you hear my last question or do you want me to…
>
> P: You asked me something about the political situation.
>
> R: Yes, how it influenced the old generation and those that had trained you.
>
> P: I don't know how they were influenced. In this time or in the past?

After some further clarifications regarding the question, the interviewer chose to ask a new question which the interviewee immediately answered. The interviewer did not dare to elaborate further as there was no opportunity to check if the interviewee only misunderstood the questions due to the bad Skype connection or if the participant deliberately avoided to answer the question. The interviewer was also informed by the fact that the interviewee previously had no trouble answering questions and as it turned out, not in the rest of the interview either. The interview pair never returned to the question at stake. Moreover, the interviewee said in the end that it would have been preferable to meet in person.

Afterwards, the interviewer wrote in the reflection note the following passage of the incidence:

> "I felt a change in the rhythm of the interview and an atmosphere of unsafety: Was I exposing her, was somebody listening? I got paranoid fantasies myself. For instance, she appeared more closed in her face and her laughter was gone for a while. Initially, she said that she had consultations by Skype abroad, so I thought she could talk freely. I started to think: Maybe it is ok to talk about personal matters on Skype but not political matters? She also mentioned in the end that it would have been much better if we had been able to meet each other instead of talking on Skype."

d) Qualitative Analyses of the Interviews

Qualitative researchers in Psychology usually limit the analysis to the subjective report of the participants (e.g., McLeod, 2013a, Polkinghorne 2005, Potter & Hepburn 2005, Rennie 2004, Smith 2004). Within psychoanalysis, a decisive assumption is that unconscious or partly unconscious defense processes distort the subjective report. This occurs particularly in the individual reports about emotionally charged processes such as psychoanalytic training. However, it is beyond the scope of the present research project to try to interpret potential unconscious processes in the interviewee.

We analyzed the interview transcriptions in two ways:

a) Qualitative content analysis;
b) Interpretative thematic analysis.

Both the content and the interpretative thematic analysis are based on team work. First the researchers analyzed their interviews individually. Subsequently, they discussed their interpretations in order to reach consensus. In this work, we have been informed by consensual qualitative research (CQR) (Hill et al., 2005, Hill, 2012), but we did not follow closely all aspects of the strict procedure. In line with the CQR-method, we have:

- used semi-structured interviews, which provide the interviewee with the possibility to express their experience and views more in their own way,

- three members of the team analyzed every interview with interpretative thematic analysis, and two with qualitative content analysis, to foster creation of multiple perspectives in the data material, and
- searched for consensus among the evaluators and description of divergences whenever divergences appeared.

McLeod (2013b, p. 366) described the intention behind CQR-research in the following way: "… to allow multiple perspectives to emerge, so that when a consensus position is reached by the group, there can be confidence that this conclusion reflects a more differentiated understanding than could be achieved by a solo researcher, and is less likely to embody an idiosyncratic or motive-driven reading of the material."

Qualitative Content Analysis

The aim of *content analysis* was to work with the text of the interview and to get insights into the interviewee's experience and perspective of their experience of their training. With content analysis we looked for themes in the narrative of the interviews – such as the experience of personal analysis, training results or social context of analytic institutions.

The method we used consisted of several steps (Graneheim & Lundman 2004). The code system covered 5 major areas (training, personal analysis, institute/society, impressions of the interview, outcome of training), split into 44 specific codes. Each code was assigned to one of the focal topics listed above. Units for coding were any uninterrupted answers in the text between two interventions of the interviewer. A unit could get, if needed, more than one code.

To shorten and concentrate the coded material, the two analysts chose relevant sentences, which conveyed the essence of the answer ("index"). The index items were subsumed under the main topic to which the index-code related. This way they created a grid (topics – indexes) which was the base of data interpretation. The index items under one topic were named "cards."

After having done the coding of the interview separately, each pair compared their coding. In case a pattern of incongruence was detected, they reviewed and identified the divergence, and looked for a consensus.

Finally, we put together the individual cards. This means the accumulation of interviews into a collected card in accordance with the main topics. More precisely if we made subgroups from the interviewees, then each subgroup had its collected card. The above created cross-sections along the focal topics of the interviews.

The qualitative content analysis provided us with a condensed version of the statements about the different topics, and with a narrative, as if the interviews had formed a common narrative.

Interpretative Thematic Analysis

In the *interpretative thematic analysis* inspired by interpretative phenomenological analysis (Finlay, 2013, McLeod, 2013a, Smith, 2004, Smith et al. 2009), the researcher pursues to make sense of the participant's attempts to make sense of their own experiences.

The themes, which in the original interpretative-analysis method are to emerge by interpretation, were already set out in our project by the foci and sub-questions in the interview guide. Our task was primarily to find out and understand the quality of experience and personal meaning of the training elements; which of them emerge as meaningful to the interviewee; and why and how are they connected to other aspects of experience and to their personality and personal circumstances.

Using the transcribed interview, each was analyzed separately by three team members. The analysis consisted of four steps:

a) During the initial reading, the analyzer took notes of first impressions and thoughts about the participants' experience with the training process and perspective on their world. This included their motives to train and their present views on the outcome. The analyst studied which themes mattered to the interviewee, why and how, and how it was related to other elements of his/her training and life.

b) Through repeated readings (after some time to let the impressions sink in and 'dream' – reflect – about them) and a constant to-and-fro between the text and the previous notes the analyst checked the original notes and comments, modified and refined them; he or she might have discovered data in other parts of the text, as well. Through the constant to-and-fro between the narrative data and the emerging thoughts the analyst made sure that the interpretations remain grounded in the words of the interviewee's narrative.
c) Evidence from the text was given to back up the themes produced by quotes from the text. The analyst made a three-column summary – explicit subjective report, interpreted meaning of the subjective report, examples – along the focal topics.
d) One of the three analysts compiled the three separate summaries into one common summary. The two others reviewed the summary; opinion divergences were discussed and resolved.

What emerged was an interpreted, condensed and restructured version of the original narrative of the interviewee's individual thinking about his or her training experience.

The type of first level end-products of the two methods is very different:

- In content analysis, the so called "cards" – a new text which contains together the answers to a certain topic as one text, in cross-sectional way
- In interpretative analysis the summaries as meanings of experience of the individual, in the wholeness of the interview.

During the elaboration of the gained secondary data, we brought the three methods (quantitative analysis of the questionnaires, qualitative content analysis, and interpretative thematic analysis) into a dialogue. We not only looked whether the results from one method underpinned or contradicted the others, but also used them to understand the results as pointers for further exploration.

III. From Analytic Practice to Training Experiences and from Training Motivation to Representational Confluence

One of our complex research goals was to gain a better understanding of the personal growth and development of psychoanalytic identity as a process during the psychoanalytic training.

To begin, we looked into the basic personal data gathered from "basic data questionnaire." We wanted to see if there was a difference between those who participated in regular training (R) and those who participated in "non-regular" training (NR).

We found no statistical difference regarding analytic practice and other formal data between the two groups of novice analysts: *age (49), psychotherapeutic practice (mean 33 years), total number of clients (from beginning mean 274), psychoanalytic practice (during training and after), and number of conducted analyses (mean 8).* According to our sample, the typical novice analyst is a middle-age practitioner with a strong history of psychotherapeutic practice who has a couple of patients in regular analysis also after completion of training (this speaks again the general view that analytic practice is disappearing). This does not depend on the type of training or on the country where he/she is working.

This first picture moved us to focus more on training *experiences,* and to look for similarities-differences; and to presume that differences group around other lines than R/NR.

Regarding the formation of psychoanalytic identity, there are subtle individual patterns of motivations, which play important roles in the choice of psychoanalysis as a profession. Different expectations and initial problems can be present at the beginning of psychoanalytic training.

We focused on the following topics:

- Personal motivation of choosing psychoanalysis as a treatment and as a profession;

- Experiences in personal training analysis and supervision and the relation between them;
- Formation of analytic identity in connection with the process of integration into the psychoanalytic milieu.

From Training Analysis Experiences

In questionnaires on personal analysis and on supervision experience, we looked for satisfaction/dissatisfaction. In the content analysis of interviews, we gathered the following themes: relationship with the analyst and supervisors; taking them for model, identification object; statements on satisfaction/dissatisfaction; expressions of positive/negative feelings toward analyst; toward supervisor; continuation of some kind/separation from analyst; from supervisor.

In the questionnaires, we found no difference between the groups R and NR regarding satisfaction with training analysis, relationship with the training analyst, or the technique of the training analyst.

To this question we used the following scales:

- training analysis satisfaction;
- attachment/dependence on training analyst;
- positive alliance;
- negative alliance;
- classical technique;
- supportive technique;
- helpful insight technique;
- positive relational qualities.

An obvious interpretation could be that the non-regular subgroup's satisfaction with training analysis and attachment to/dependence on the training analyst is not significantly higher or lower than that of the "regulars"; neither do they develop a significantly stronger or weaker positive or negative alliance with their training analyst.

There was only one statistical difference: the "non-regular" subgroup members scored their analysts on the "positive personality scale" significantly higher than the "regulars" ($t(51)=2{,}12$ $p<0{,}05$).

Possible interpretations of the above could be:

- due to the exceptional situation (and higher investment), shuttle analysts were more engaged than usual into the endeavor;
- due to the exceptional situation (and higher investment), the shuttling candidates were more engaged and perceived the analysts to be warmer, friendlier and happier than they were;
- due to the positive evaluation of the guest culture, the candidates viewed their analysts as warmer, friendlier and happier;

The content analysis of the interviews showed that – in the whole sample – more love and positive feelings were experienced (expressed) toward the supervisor, whilst more ambivalence and resentment exhibited toward the personal analyst.

It was also observed that non-regularly trained analysts expressed satisfaction and positive feelings openly, while ambivalences and dissatisfactions regarding both personal analysts and supervisors remained hidden.

A possible interpretation of differences might be that

- on one hand, the supervision channels personal analytical experiences to professional competencies. On the other hand, the relationship with the supervisor might form a long-term collegial bond without any difficulties.
- The personal analyst often becomes a particular (therefore a beloved) object, which obviously cannot meet expectations. The unfulfilled longing causes strongly ambivalent feelings toward the psychoanalysis, as well.

- Furthermore, the candidate is more able to evaluate professional qualities of the supervisor during training than the analyst.
- To develop a collegial relationship with the training analyst or the supervisor post qualification is often not given for those trained in non-regular setting. Therefore, separation due to ending training might have a different quality for them.

Psychoanalytic Identity

We checked whether training-analysis satisfaction correlated with other factors, especially with supervision satisfaction and the developed analytic competence[7].

Our findings showed:

- Training-analysis satisfaction correlates with "attachment to / dependence on the training analyst" (*r = 0,765 p<0,001 – strong correlation),* but shows no statistical correlation with analytic competence, creativity, or analytic autonomy. In other words: based on self-reports, satisfaction with the analytic experience is not hugely connected with factors important to analytic work.
- On other hand, positive correlation is to be found amongst such factors as creativity, strategic analytic knowledge, analytic autonomy, receptive attitude, and analytic strength. All of these are important components of analytic competence.
- Creativity does not correlate with positive or negative alliance with the analyst, or with positive personality qualities of the analyst.
- Openness in supervision correlates with satisfaction in supervision, which might indicate that being open in supervision leads to better use of supervision.

[7] (For compared scales and results see Appendix).

In the content analysis of the interviews, we studied analytic-identity experience along two dimensions:

- in connection with professional functioning, with functioning in professional milieu, and with vision of future;
- exploring personal professional strengths and weaknesses.

Research findings showed that

- Two thirds of the 21 interviewees expressed strong and balanced psychoanalytic identity after (0-7 years) graduation.
- One third of the participants expressed uncertainty or ambivalence regarding analytic identity, some of them felt real mental burden concerning the question.

It became apparent that, with one exception, all from the weak analytic-identity group came from small psychoanalytic societies or study groups, and, in many cases, the existence of a peer (case discussion) group was the mediator of positive integration.

Representational Confluence between Personal Analyst and Supervisor

In addition to differences between satisfaction with training analyst and with supervisor, we checked whether the thematic interpretative analysis of the interviews reinforced those differences.

Our analysis procedure followed a permanent sequence: First, we went through the whole "interpretation" column (that means we incorporated all topics together into one text). Then, we extracted the parts that related to the analyst or the supervisor as a role model or idealized object. Finally, we grouped them into different types.

Although supervision satisfaction seemed to be more matured than satisfaction with the training analysis according to the interpretative analysis, relational aspects played a more important role than expected.

Unsurprisingly, training analysts very often became “love objects for life.” *What surprised us was that one or the other of the supervisors of the candidate also took up this role – either as the continuation of personal analysis or instead of the training analyst.* The same pattern appeared in the content analysis, as well.

The intensity of the descriptions and the formulations differed from interview to interview (from clear statements to half-hidden idealization or modeling). It seemed important that *one of the three* (the training analyst or one of the supervisors) functioned that way. In some cases the training analyst was idealized, but the supervisor was viewed as role model. Additionally, we often found continuation in the internal representation.

This *personal confluence* did not depend on the regular-non-regular type of training.

The philosophy of analytic training is aimed at keeping apart personal analysis and supervision so that neither would “take the place of the other.” Nevertheless, this can only be fulfilled within limits, because it cannot be consciously controlled (“take this to your personal analysis, this has no place here”, or “you are not in supervision here”). On a deeper level, the analyst and the supervisor are more or less in fusion as the representative of psychoanalysis, and the idealized object – as a continuum and replacement of each other.

The representational confluence of analyst and supervisor leads our attention to the question of motivation before and when choosing analytic training. We looked at the beginnings of training: what are the motives and how do they influence the decision to go into analysis and the wish to become an analyst Moreover, we became interested in how those internal objects (analyst-supervisor) persist after training termination, how they form analytic identity, and how they transform along the integration into the analytic milieu.

Examples on confluence along the three major different groups of findings:

Master-apprentice coincidence – similarity of working style, personal presence, and quality giving safety: *“I think I identified with both – with my training analyst and with this supervision, because I think they were rather similar in their work. And so a good... addition." "It was chained together – analysis and supervision."*

Maturation process in the supervision – "now I understand my analysis": *"I never got the feeling that I fully explored my deeper issues in my analysis. That was something that I mostly developed, paradoxically, in my supervision a little bit, because my first supervision included a great deal of personal work also."*

Loss in analysis – reparation in supervision: *"It was the first supervisor who has given the acceptance and attention I missed in analysis."*

Personal Motivations When Choosing Psychoanalysis

What are the motivations for entering into psychoanalytic training? To study this issue, we collected the statements from subtopic motivation in content analysis of the interviews and compared them with motivational statements from the interpretative analysis.

Entering into the psychoanalytic training, the desire of "getting healed" and of "becoming a professional" are both present as primary motivations. The wish for "getting healed" is stronger and more profound; one of the components of this wish is the belief that one will get rid of all of his sickness. The guarantee of this is that one will belong to the "chosen" ones. This wish is manifested by the conviction of having chosen the "best" analyst.

Our results showed three different motivational backgrounds:

To get rid of personal pains and difficulties:

A group of participants expressed a strong wish to be able to solve difficult childhood relationships, chronic depressions, and emotional imbalances. Quite a few expressed to have significant emotional pain and difficulty as part of primary motivation when entering personal analysis.

This group of the interviewees reported to have had long lasting suffering due to parental death and losses. They experienced early separation from their native country and culture, losing languages. They also suffered from the impact of trans-generational traumas. In many cases, loneliness and fear of rejection, helplessness, and weakness occurred in the background surrounded by tense atmosphere. These individuals often come from families with a history of aggression, including the impact of mental diseases in the family, as well as suicide, and suicide attempts.

Curiosity about oneself and for others in a helping way:

Another group of participants spoke more of curiosity about oneself and for others in a helping way. They reported to have had an early interest in dreams, curiosity about the human psyche, or an interest in gaining a deeper understanding of the nature of human existence. They gained positive experiences from their childhood concerning their capacity to listen to people, and felt that they had the ability to contain others' problems as helpers.

Being recognized, to be part of a highly valued group - analysis promises to belong "to another world":

The wish to be recognized and become part of a highly valued group also appeared, in different forms. As part of primary motivation, this covered what psychoanalysis "promised" for the future trainee: among other things it promised protection, symbolized in the desire: *"I am not going to be sick or ill, if I become an analyst."* This idealization regarding the psychoanalytic profession could be connected with a strong fear of rejection, and it might be understood, as "I could be never healed." Those who belonged to this group expressed a stronger wish to belong to professionals who provide support and empathy. They had fear of rejection, and formulated their wish to be recognized as a professional. Many of them had an early encounter with Freud's writings, and showed interest in his psychoanalytic world. In this group of participants, falling in love with a person who was an analyst and falling in love with the professional field also presented itself as a motivational background.

Interestingly, there were participants in the project who avoided disclosure of any information on their primary motivations regarding their choice of psychoanalysis as treatment or as a profession. Their wish or personal background was not possible to explore, their answers were often incomprehensible, and the statements given to the interviewer's questions were ambiguous or generalized concerning the topic of motivation.

Formation of Analytic Identity in Connection with the Process of Integration into the Psychoanalytic Society

For a trainee, becoming a psychoanalyst and belonging to the psychoanalytic community might promise fulfillment; it does not only mean to belong to an elite, but what we call "relieving from the position of being ill." The institute might also become the subject of idealization, ambivalence and disappointment. The ambivalence may appear as a split between "good analysts" and "horrible ones," and in the expectation of being perfect as an analytical society contrary to other similar societies.

Evaluating the possible reasons of such differences concerning hiding positions and the open attitudes of the analyst, we were interested in how the different motivational patterns connect to:

1) The strength of psychoanalytic identity;
2) the attitudes of analysts toward their psychoanalytic environment and society;
3) the experiences in and confluences between personal analysis and supervision.

Psychoanalytic identity was examined along two main topics in the interviews:

- Activity in professional life and expressed plans for the future as analyst
- Experiences of personal strengths and weaknesses being an analyst.

Research findings showed that:

- More than two thirds of the participants expressed to have a strong and balanced psychoanalytic identity after (0-7 years) graduation.
- One third of the participants expressed uncertainty or ambivalence regarding analytic identity, some of them felt real difficulties concerning the question.

It became apparent, with one exception that all participants from the *weak analytic identity group* came from small psychoanalytic societies or study groups, and, in many cases the existence of a peer (case discussion) group was the mediator of positive integration. However, the sample is too small to draw final consequences.

An Example for the Composition of Motivation – Confluence – Identity Formation/Integration

Motivation: the analyst connects her motivation to her childhood where she felt alone. She felt loneliness to her subsequent emotional need to repair her parents. Choice of political activity in early adult years, this political view was anti-psychoanalytic. Felt "pain in her existence" and problems in her love relations.

Confluence: she had an utopist wish and longing for an idealized society and to become one of the ideal people. The first analyst was a "difficult one", but she remained inside. The second analyst was a true love for her. Disappointment: as if the analyst wanted to get rid of her (like from an affair).

Analyst and supervisors together, amalgamated became the role model – the internal analyst – for her. She gained a lot from her analyses and from her supervisions, so the influence has been very clear and great.

As if psychoanalysis would be her life from birth and she would be reborn through analysis/training as another, a free person. Personal analysts, supervisors but also seminar leader flow together into one beloved object – became part of her.

Identity: Her aspiration in the psychoanalytic society today is to be able to speak truly and she feels that her colleagues allow her to do it. She describes psychoanalysis as a "world with a lot of power" in all other parts of the society, and she does not like these dynamics. Power struggle between Kleinians and psychoanalysts is regular. Ambivalence in what psychoanalysis represents for her.

IV. The Role of Institutional Dynamics and Social Context of Psychoanalytic Organizations

Exploration of the role of institutional dynamics and wider social context was not part of the initial design of the study. However, before the data collection started, and due to the experience of the research group members, their strong impact of this two factors on the life of psychoanalytic organizations was recognized. As a result, the interview focal points and the procedures of the qualitative methods were enriched with three new topics – institutional culture, leadership, and role of the social context. The choice of these three is in line with the psychoanalytic approach to organizational life, which usually includes exploration of the interrelatedness between anxieties and primary tasks, structures, culture, leadership, and social defences of the institution (Obholzer, 1986; Trist & Murray, 1990).

The essence of content analysis of the present topics was to find and code every part of the transcripts related to the institutional culture, leadership and the impact of the social context and subsequently, to comment how the interviewees experienced them in relation to their integration to local analytic society. In the interpretative thematic analysis, researchers also analyzed these topics and interpreted their possible sources and interrelatedness.

We formulated two research questions:

a) Are members of the European institutes aware of institutional dynamics and do they have sufficient leadership skills to counterbalance the effects of traumatic history and local culture?
b) Are there differences in the institutional life of Western and Eastern European psychoanalytic societies?

We hypothesized that:

a) The overall satisfaction with training institutes will be similar in both the Western European (regular training) and the Eastern European (non-regular) group, but the attitude towards the society of the non-regular group will be more ambivalent;
b) Psychoanalytic institutes in former totalitarian countries would be more vulnerable to primitive organizational dynamics due to insufficiently integrated democratic and psychoanalytic values and the impact of traumatic experiences.

Institutional Culture

The term institutional culture encompasses organizational values and behaviors that contribute to the unique social and psychological environment of an organization. It represents the mission, norms, beliefs, language and symbols of organizational members and is a result of the characteristics of its history, working task, leadership, as well as cultural and political context. It is usually described as strong or weak, participatory or authoritarian. *Strong institutional culture* exists where members respond to stimulus because of their identification with organizational values. In cases of *weak culture,* there is little alignment with organizational values, and control must be exercised through extensive bureaucracy. Organizations should strive for what is considered strong organizational culture in order to increase development, growth, efficiency, and reduce counterproductive behavior of their members. One division which highly corresponds to definitions of weak and strong, but relevant to psychoanalytic organization, is between *participatory* and *authoritarian* institutional cultures. Participatory culture encourages various members of the organization to take a leadership role. Signs of lack of participatory culture surface when leadership is personified and permanently associated with the managerial role. Authoritarian culture is often found to serve as social defense against anxiety of chaos and failure. Research (Menzies Lyth, 1960; 1988) suggests that authoritarian institutional cultures have destructive effects both on the personality of the members and on organizational life because of the dehumanization, depersonalization, and bureaucratization of organizational functioning. On the other hand, participatory (strong, healthy) organizational cultures provide benefits, such as effective leadership, organizational behavior and team cohesiveness, high morale and strong identification with the humanism, goals, and ethic of psychoanalysis.

The interviewees of our study commented experiences they considered to have both positive and negative aspects of the institutional life of their psychoanalytic organizations.

The following dynamics were regarded to have positive impact on organizational integrity, their commitment and professional identity:

- Tolerance of different positions and psychoanalytic theories;
- The IPA Sponsoring Committees are experienced as a protective structure against conflicts in society;
- Establishment of informal groups, e.g., intervision groups may function as a defensive structure in situations of conflicts in the local organization;

The following dynamics were experienced as having negative impact and to lead to increased distance of the interviewees from their psychoanalytic organizations:

Existence of power struggles and destructive competition:

"The first wave, the generation before me, was very violent, it was very much a time of struggles with many personal attacks. ... The main thing that prompted me to leave (the society and the country) was the sensation that, even though I and my colleagues were very energetic and we had many ideas, it was not possible actually to make a difference. Or, I personally did not find the way."

- The process of group development is not stable, but fluctuates with many ups and downs;
- Deeply disturbing boundary violations occur, such as love affairs and clashes between the individual training analyst and the supervisor;
- Self-marginalization of the institute/society and its candidates;

For example, one of the interviewees stated: "*I feel that our psychoanalytic, this classical psychoanalytic community, is quite encapsulated!*"

We want to emphasize that when these aspects of institutional culture are prominent, some members leave not only their psychoanalytic society, but also their country of origin.

Leadership

Psychoanalytic theories about leadership are developed with considerable depth by Wilfred Bion (Bion, 1961). He defined leadership not in terms of individual leader, but as a group function which embodies equilibrium between emotions and reason, and between individual and social, and thus, facilitates healthy organizational development (Torres, 2013). Two types of dysfunctional leadership pathology that need special attention are authoritarianism and narcissism. Authoritarian leadership implies rigid and excessive force to maintain control over organizational processes. Narcissistic leadership involves grandiose aspirations about image and display, but easily loses track of the difference between fantasy and reality and is liable to dramatic failures (Gabriel, 2011).

An impressive finding in our study is that questions about leadership were rarely mentioned or answered by the interviewees in either non-regular or regular groups. Nevertheless, the concept of leadership was strikingly absent in most non-regular interviews. More importantly, despite having been included in the final design of the interviews as a focal point it stayed a topic that was rarely asked by the interviewers. When leadership was discussed, participants considered the following aspects as having positive impact on institutional life:

- Ability of analysts to collaborate and support activities of others;
- Capacity of taking formal or informal roles in society;
- Desire to become training analyst and to lead seminars.

The general impression was that most of the participants did not consider themselves to have knowledge and leadership skills and they experienced difficulties in taking leadership roles, or even refused to do so. The defensive stance was sometimes prevailing, but in other cases the concepts itself was lacking to the point of interviewees stating: *"I do not understand your question!"*

The attitude towards leadership differed considerably between participants from Western and Eastern Europe. For example an Eastern-European interviewee stated: *"Leadership is not a very clear issue. It's a little muddy!",* while a Western-European participant shared that: *"I am also involved in the institutional work of our society. So, I do believe in the treatment of the patient, but I also believe in the institution of psychoanalysis. Because I believe these two things go together."*

It could be hypothesized that part of the reason why leadership in Eastern Europe is experienced in such split terms can be related to the inner image of parental and authority figures. There are extreme cases when corruption of the social and political system affects not only the inner perception of psychoanalytical institution, but the mind of respondents: *...nothing could hold me and that provoked a lot of suffering inside."*

Consequently, some of the participants felt that they could not develop further in their home country, and moved to parts of the world with established democratic and psychoanalytic traditions.

Impact of the Social Context

Participants from both regular and non-regular societies rarely discussed the possible influence of being part of a totalitarian society and how that impacted the life of individuals or institutions. When asked, it became clear that some of them were not aware or preferred to be oblivious about possible inter-relatedness:

"You asked me something about the political situation… I don't know how they were influenced. "

"... in A it was so huge striving to be independent and to fight with the B, C and D. I think the real problem is (that) we have the model of being victims. This victim is so huge and is still so hungry. I hate it!"

There was a small group of respondents who stated that they were very well aware of how their past–was putting a shadow on their present life. These interviewees were investing serious effort to break the authoritarian social norms that fueled life of their analytic societies, and actively tried to overcome their own passivity and to avoid adopting the role of a victim. They considered that life in such societies taught them not only to accept but to overcome limitations. As result of this experience, they were trying to promote psychoanalysis and its values in the wider society. However, the majority of the participants stated that certain characteristic of their local culture were experienced as hostile, so they doubted that their training could be ensured economically. In addition, they considered psychoanalysis to be ignored by the general public in their countries and the prevailing attitude of the pharmaceutical industry, psychiatry and other psychotherapeutic schools is denigrating and aggressive. They shared worries that the poor economy and traumatic history would influence functioning of their psychoanalytic societies, and they conveyed lack of skills to minimize or prevent it.

"I'm fighting a lot in our group... Sometimes I think that it is also connected with my parents' past ... and the structure of training institutions - it marginalizes candidates."

The Arch from Motivation through Training Experience to Integration into the Society

The results of the interpretative thematic analysis show three main variations regarding motivation-confluence-integrity and psychoanalytic identity formation:

1) One third of the participants showed *stable identity without sufficient integration* into the psychoanalytic society: these participants had positive experiences regarding intense motivation at the beginning, significant confluence between analyst and supervisor and stable identity formation, but their integration into psychoanalytic community was insufficient.
2) Another third of the participants reported *weak analytic identity and difficult integration* into psychoanalytic community: this group expressed ambivalent or no motivation, weak confluence between personal analysis and supervision, difficulties in analytic-identity formation, and troublesome belonging to psychoanalytic society.

Examples:

- The situation in the country is very troublesome and traumatic, being a victim must be the general social role model where she is living. The real problem in the psychoanalytic society was that they had the model of being victims.

- There were fights in the society about the positions; it was hard to understand why the society was so straight towards their own member and candidate.

3) The last third of the interviewees had *strong identity with strong commitment* to the psychoanalytic society: this group consisted of participants who had strong primary motivations at the beginning, experienced significant confluence between personal analyst and supervision, gained stable identity formation, and developed strong commitment to the analytic society.

Examples:

- Participant started to function as leader of theoretical seminars for analytic training in her society;
- Willing to become both a training analyst and a supervisor in the future;
- The respondent is also part of a group who reads articles and discusses them and this is a creative experience for her;
- Having a role as a person who transmits psychoanalytic competence to next generations;
- Quite involved in thinking about training matters and organizational development;
- The interviewee is very convincing about her experience of being helped by her analysis, and this seems a very solid basis to her wish to train and function as a psychoanalyst.

V. Conclusion: What Do Our Findings Say to the Debates on Analytic Training?

To date, there has not been sufficient data of regular trainings regarding training experiences, competences at qualification, and the application of obtained analytic competence in later practice provided by traditional analytic training institutes. Therefore, this project brings important results for all involved in psychoanalytic education (such as candidates, trainers, training institutes, and society executives) regardless whether they are engaged in regular or non-regular trainings. In the PIEE and, during the early years of newly founded study groups/societies in Eastern Europe, shuttle analysis/shuttle training existed besides regular education settings.

We expected to gain more clarity on psychoanalytic education in different training settings. Setting here refers both to the form of training (regular and shuttle), and to the institutional environment (established-traditional institutes exceptionally structured and pioneer phase ones). We contemplated whether the various training settings prompted differences in the sense of analytic competence and practice (analytic career); or whether those differences could be found more within the training experiences and in the way in which the transformation to becoming an analyst takes place or occurs.

We hoped to get a clearer picture whether the investments (of trainees, trainers and institutions-organizations) are appropriate, higher or lower than what the "production" of analysts would require. We also expected to find out more about how analytic training is converted into professional practice in our times. From the above we sought to understand more why it is worth to start analytic training. Additionally, we aimed to learn more about the experience of regular training, which can be compared with other new training experiments in the future.

Based on the subjective reports of the participating graduate psychoanalysts, an overview of the data material from the questionnaires and the interviews does not support the notion that psychoanalytic training in regular and non-regular settings may result in substantial differences in psychoanalytic competencies, psychoanalytic identity formation, or in psychoanalytic practice after graduation. On the contrary, the striking result is the similarities in training outcomes between the two groups. Likewise, it is not the comparison between the two training types that seems to influence the participants' awareness of negative institutional dynamics and leadership problems and their willingness to participate in organizational work.

These findings promoted a change in the primary focus in our study to experiences of training in general. In the data analysis regarding this issue, so far, we have explored motivation to start training and an apparent confluence between attachment to psychoanalytic training and psychoanalysis as such, the personal analyst, and at least one supervisor.

An already experienced professional's wish to start training could also be related to the combined motivation of healing ("getting rid of all pains forever") and to becoming a member of a highly valued profession as therapist for others. This helps to understand why middle aged, professionally advanced people start psychoanalytic training, and also calls to revisit the importance of healing motivation when someone chooses analytic training and to build in that aspect positively into the "marketing" of psychoanalysis.

According to our data, the non-regular subgroup's satisfaction with training analysis and attachment/dependence on the training analyst is not significantly higher or lower than that of the "regulars"; neither do they develop a significantly stronger or weaker alliance with the analyst. However, "non-regulars" rated the personality of the training analyst higher than "regulars." This might be due to both the analyst and the candidate's greater investment in the shuttle setting. It could also be driven by the exceptional circumstances under which the meetings took place. Namely, the participants being outside their home environment and being introduced to a different culture.

Satisfaction with personal analysis shows statistical correlation with attachment to -dependence on the training analyst. Nonetheless, it does not correspond with a recognized level of achieved competence. We suppose that there is an indirect connection between personal analysis satisfaction and its effects on analytic competence. The philosophy of analytic training aims to separate personal analysis and supervision so that neither would "take the place of the other." Nevertheless, this is only possible to fulfill within limits. Our findings validate the assumption that on a deeper level, the analyst and the supervisor are more or less in fusion as the representative of psychoanalysis and the idealized object, as a continuum and replacement of one another. It was obvious in the interviews that many aspects of personal analysis are continued in supervision. Elements and feelings, which inherently belong to personal analysis, re-occur as unprocessed issues in the supervision, thus, giving space to further elaboration and reparation work.

The extent of confluence of internal representation between the psychoanalytic profession, personal analyst, supervisor, and analytic movement/society suggests to revisit the interplay of personal analysis and supervision in training (the separation of personal analysis and supervision and its unfeasibility). It also indicates that personal analysis and supervision complete each other.

The results of interpretative and content analysis of the interviews show that there are great amounts of satisfaction and dissatisfaction linked to the different phases of psychoanalytic training. Despite the composition of these positive and negative experiences, all of the interviewees maintain psychoanalytic practice after graduation. This means that they gained those good and bad objects, which finally result in acquiring the capacity of bearing ambivalence and overcoming the idealization of the psychoanalytic profession, identity, and the analytic society.

In the process of confluence, the complexity of significant role models contributes to developing and attaining psychoanalytic attitude and knowledge. The subtle balance between integration and distraction from them

- leads the individual psychoanalysts to find their own psychoanalytic voice and identity during training;
- helps to understand more the strength of analytic identity (compared with other psychotherapies – to be a true analyst);
- underlines that the training tempo is individual and that way conflicting with school-class systems; a good balance should be found;
- and makes understandable why analytic training has unavoidably a surplus over learning a method.

The result of the interpretative thematic analysis about dissatisfaction and poor integration to local psychoanalytic organizations in two thirds of all interviewees needs special consideration. This finding cannot be explained only as a result of the paradox inherited in personal psychoanalysis. Berman (1998) discussed that both personal psychoanalysis and analytic education could unlock creative potential, but they also had regressive and paranoid tendencies. Our study confirmed the findings of previous authors (Kernberg, 1996; 2016; Ward et al, 2010) who found certain levels of idealization and paranoia, regarding outcomes of the training in the experience of their respondents. Therefore, the main task of the members of training committees remains not to encourage regressive tendencies, and to oppose the utopian fantasy of a purified new person by following current ethical standards and available data about what the realistic requirements are for analytic candidates, personal analysts, supervisors, and trainers (Fonagy & Target, 1997; Varvin, 2003).

It is worth to consider the fact that Eastern European institutes are in a more vulnerable position, and they need considerable attention and inputs in terms of organizational consultancy and leadership training. In order to counterbalance these regressive tendencies, we need to intervene both on an international and on a local level. Such interventions can take the form of new studies on organizational life, public debates on possible effects of traumatic experiences on our institutes, incorporation of topics about groups, institutions and social dynamics in our training and post-graduate curriculums, etc. There is an urgent need for new policies about the effects of socio-cultural factors on psychoanalytic organizations and for the implementation of leadership training for psychoanalysts in Europe.

The exploration of organizational dynamics shows certain pitfalls of European training systems. The first major finding is that the circumstantial institutional and social context significantly influenced all interviewees. Generally, our respondents conveyed sensitivity to institutional problems, but rarely appeared to have sufficient knowledge and leadership skills to introduce necessary changes at the organizational level.

Our study shows that the PIEE contributed significantly to the development of psychoanalysis in Eastern Europe. It served as a socializing agent and model for the new study groups/societies and provided a model for transmitting not only IPA standards but also democratic principles and values in general to new areas worldwide. The PIEE gave more than what traditional institutes usually would – for example nurturing of would be new analytic groups. Our study also supports the importance of analytic organizations and peer case discussion groups.

We are aware that participants of our study were newly qualified analysts and that the experiences of those who are well integrated into the profession could be different. Our findings need to be viewed as preliminary exploration of the organizational life of European psychoanalytic institutions. Additional studies with more complex designs need to be conducted in the near future.

The experience of the developed Skype-interview method adds to the ongoing debate within the psychoanalytic tradition about the use of new technologies in personal analysis and supervision and now in research. The use of Skype enabled the present research project with participating psychoanalysts from all over Eastern and Western Europe. It would not have been possible to conduct the project otherwise, due to travel expenses. The weakness of the method is the restricted ability for the interview pair to relate to each other compared to a face-to-face meeting, which additionally, may have compensated more for the language barrier as neither the interviewees nor the interviewers were native English speakers. It however seems that the personal commitment of the interviewees to the research project partly counteracted this limitation.

Another issue has been the ethical aspects of using Skype for interviews addressing such a private and intimate matter as psychoanalytic training. Part of the research design's mandate has been to instigate procedures in order to secure participants' anonymity as much as possible and to hinder data leakage. Moreover, psychoanalysts are particularly capable research participants. It is our view that they are able to assess the risks of participating compared to the potential outcome of the research.

What are the consequences of potential surveillance of online interviewing? Can we defend the use of online-technology in research within psychoanalysis? Skype is already in use in psychoanalytic treatment and supervision, but this activity has lately been in the focus of discussions within the IPA. The research group has discussed the issue on several occasions.

Churcher (2015) has put forth objections to online practice within psychoanalysis. He strongly recommended that we do not give into the temptation of using online technology for psychoanalytic treatment and supervision despite its convenience through allowing communication that would otherwise be impossible. His arguments are also relevant for online interviews.

Churcher characterizes analysts as naïve who puts forth that clinical data is not interesting to others than the analyst pair or that these data is not understandable to outsiders as naïve. He also believes that outsiders would not understand what is going on, say the least, learn anything from it. He fears that this argumentation is an instance of "turning a blind eye" to the dangers, both in respect of violating the necessary security in the consulting room (here the research room), and of the potential vast misuse of confidential information in the case of unfriendly persons or regimes potentially gaining access now or later.

We ask if such a position is too dogmatic, as if there is only a "yes-or-no" answer to the use of online technology. Instead, our research group will advocate a more flexible approach, taking into consideration all sorts of aspects that may add to the overall potential harm to the interviewee if someone to gain unpermitted access to the data.

In particular, there is a need to consider the participants' ability to understand the consequences of taking part in online-interviews. Graduate psychoanalysts in Europe constitute a highly selected sample with a level of education that makes them particularly able to understand the consequences of Skype interviewing. As a result of their professional training, we can expect them to be more aware of the type of data offered than others. Moreover, due to their historical background, Eastern-European participants in particular, have the ability to confront the surveillance fear, as we must assume that they have reflected extensively about the issue before. It is interesting that none of the interviewees, Eastern or Western psychoanalysts alike, used the opportunity in the end of the interview to question the Skype situation and consequently, potential ethical challenges.

Additionally, if someone illegally monitors the conversation or if the Skype administration or others publish the conversation unpermitted, they commit criminal acts. In our opinion, we cannot fully defend ourselves against such activities. After all, our data does not contain military or economical secrets.

When having such competent participants as newly graduated psychoanalysts, we must respectfully allow them to consider for themselves the risk of participation against the potential benefits. Our participants appeared to greatly identify with the topic of the research. They shared their experiences in order to promote the knowledge and understanding of training processes. This argumentation is in line with the argumentation for Skype analytic and supervision sessions given to Eastern-European psychoanalysts during breaks in their shuttle analysis and supervision. Today, as a result of this shuttle training, there are psychoanalytic institutes and societies in almost all countries in Eastern Europe, offering regular training to their new candidates.

The topic of online research calls for nuances. We have ended with an approval of online research within limits. Online technology must be considered individually in each new project, including technological developments that further limit access to the research data. Researchers should take into consideration the ability of the participants to understand the consequences of their participation, the political context of the research now and in the future, and to assess the potential benefits of the research against the costs. Instead of disavowing all online technology altogether, we should take part in the new possibilities online technology offer. We need experiences that make us able to further refine the procedures and the ethical standards of this kind of methodology within psychoanalysis.

The intense emotions evoked in the interviewees also evoked counter-transference feelings in the interviewers, instigating a reflection process that was presented in their written reports after each interview. They each interviewed five participants and after several years, the interviews are still present in their mind. This reaction supports the trustworthiness of the data, and that the interviewees in the Skype situation were able to convey significant experiences in their training. In sum, it is our conclusion that by using Skype-interviewing we received sufficient data to use as fundamental material for training research focusing on broad patterns in the various elements of the training experience of psychoanalytic candidates.

REFERENCES

Berman, E. (1998). Structure and Individuality in Psychoanalytic Training: The Israeli Controversial Discussions. *Am. J. Psychoanal., 58*,117-133.

Bion, W. (1961). *Learning from Experience.* London: Tavistock.

Bollas, C., & Diatkine, G. (2010). Shuttle Analysis in the Han-Prakken Psychoanalytic Institute for Eastern Europe (PIEE). *Int. J. Psycho-Anal., 91*, 1250-1253.

Bush, M., & William, M. (2011). Should supportive measures and relational variables be considered a part of psychoanalytic technique? *Intern. J. Psychoanal., 92,* 377-399.

Cabaniss, D.L., Glick, R.A., & Roose, S.P. (2001). The Columbia Supervision Project: Data from the Dyad. *J. Amer. Psychoanal. Assn.*, 235-267.

Chucher, J. (2015). Privacy, Telecommunications and the Psychoanalytic Setting. Panel presentation at the EPF congress in Stockholm.

Deakin, H., & Wakefield, K. (2014). Skype interviewing: Reflections of two PhD researchers. *Qualitative Research*, *14,* 603-616.

Eike, H. (2015): What do we learn in psychoanalytic training? *Intern. J. Psychoanal., 96,* 755-771.

Filet, B., Szőnyi, G. (2009). Do psychoanalytic competencies have specific features? Results of a pilot study. *Intern. J. Psychother., 13*, 21-33.

Finlay, L. (2011). Interpretative phenomenological analysis. In L. Finlay (Ed.), *Phenomenology for Therapists, Phenomenological Research Approaches*, 139-147. Chichester: John Wiley & Sons.

Fonagy, P., & Target, M. (1997). Attachment and reflective function: their role in self-organization. *Devel. Psychol.*, *9,* 679-700.

Fonagy, P. (2003)., Some complexities in the relationship of psychoanalytic theory to technique. *Psychoanalytic Quarterly, 72*, 13-47.

Fonagy, P. (2006). The failure of practice to inform theory and the role of implicit theory in bridging the transmission gap. In: Canestri, J. ed.: *Psychoanalysis: From practice to theory*. London: Wiley, 69-86.

Gabriel, Y. (2011). Psychoanalytic approaches to leadership. In A. Bryman, D. Collinson, K. *The SAGE Handbook of Leadership*, Sage, Thousand Oaks

Graneheim, U.H., & Lundman, B. (2004). Qualitative content analysis in nursing research: concepts, procedures and measures to achieve trustworthiness. *Nurse Education Today, 24*, 105-112.

Grint, B. Jackson, & M. Uhl-Bien (Eds.), *The SAGE Handbok of Leadership.* 393-405. London: Sage.

Hill, C.E. (Ed.) (2012). *Consensual qualitative research: A practical resource for investigating social science phenomena.* Washington DC: American Psychological Association.

Hill, C.E., Knox, S., Thompson, B.J., Williams, E.N., Hess, S.A., & Ladany, N. (2005). Consensual qualitative research: An update. *Journal of Counseling Psychology, 52*, 196-205.

Janghorban, R. et al. (2014). Skype interviewing: The new generation of online synchronous interview in qualitative research. *International Journal of Qualitative Studies on Health and Well-being,* 9: 1-3.

Kernberg, O.F. (1996). Thirty methods to destroy the creativity of psychoanalytic candidates. *Intern. J. Psychoanal., 77*, 1031-1040.

Kernberg, O.F. (2016). *Psychoanalytic Education at the Crossroads*: *Reformation, change and the future of psychoanalytic training*, New York: The New Library of Psychoanalysis, *R*outledge.

Killingmo, B. (1995). Affirmation in psychoanalysis. *International journal of psychoanalysis, 76*, 503-518.

Killingmo, B. (2006). A plea for affirmation. Relating to states of unmentalised affects. *Scandinavian psychoanalytic review, 29*(1), 13-21.

Kvale, S. (1996). *Interviews: An introduction to qualitative research interviewing*. Thousand Oaks: Sage Publications.

McLeod, J. (2013a). Qualitative research: Methods and contributions. In M. J. Lambert (Ed.), *Begin and Garfield's handbook of Psychotherapy and behavior change* (6th ed.). New Jersey: John Wiley & Sons.

McLeod, J. (2013b). Consensual qualitative research: A practical resource for investigating social science phenomena. *Psychotherapy Research, 23*, 366-367.

Menzies Lyth, I. (1960). A case-study in the functioning of social systems as a defence against anxiety. A report on a study of the nursing service of a general hospital. *Human Relations. 13,* 95-121.

Menzies Lyth, I. (1988). *Containing Anxiety in Institutions, Vol. 1.* London: Free Association Books.

Obholzer, A. (1986). Institutional Dynamics and Resistance to Change. *Psychoanal. Psychother., 2,* 201-206;

Ortega, L. R. (2017). *Integrating family therapy and play therapy: Perspectives and experiences of family counselors.* (Ph.D.), Barry University. (AAI10109069)

Polkinghorne, D.E. (2005). Language and meaning: Data collection in qualitative research. *Journal of Counseling Psychology, 52***,** 137-145.

Potter, J., & Hepburn, A. (2005). Qualitative interviews in psychology: Problems and possibilities. *Qualitative Research in Psychology, 2*, 281-307.

Rennie, D.L. (2004). Anglo-north American qualitative counseling and psychotherapy research. *Psychotherapy Research*, *14*, 37-55.

Seitz, S. (2016). Pixilated partnerships, overcoming obstacles in qualitative interviews via Skype: A research note. *Qualitative Research, 16*(2), 229-235.

Smith, J.A., Flowers, P., & Larkin, M. (2009). *Interpretative phenomenological analysis: Theory, method and analysis*. London: Sage.

Strømme, H., Gullestad, S.E., Stänicke, E., & Killingmo, B. (2010). A widening scope on therapist development. A research interview informed by psychoanalysis. *Qualitative research in psychology, 7*(3), 214-232.

Sullivan, J.R. (2012). Skype: An appropriate method of data collection for qualitative interviews? *The Hilltop Review*, *6(1),* Article 10, 53-60.

Szőnyi, G., & Stájner-Popovič, T. (2008). Shuttle analysis, shuttle supervision and shuttle life — some facts, experiences and questions. *Psychoanalytic Inquiry, 28,* 309-328.

Torres, N. (2013). *The psycho-social field dynamics: Kurt Lewin and Wilfred Bion*, In N. Torres & R. Hinshelwood (Eds.), Bion's Sources: Shifting of his paradigm: 68-79. London: Routledge.

Trist, E., & Murray, H. (1990). *The social engagement of social science. A Tavistock Anthology. Vol. l The Socio-psychological perspective,* Eric Trist & Hugh Murray (Eds.) Philadelphia: University of Pennsylvania Press 1990.

Tuckett, D. (2005). Does anything go? Towards a framework for the more transparent assessment of psychoanalytic competence. *Intern. J. Psychoanal., 86*: 31-49.

Ward, A., Gibson, W. and Miqueu-Baz, C. (2010). Between Paranoia and Creativity: Candidates' Experience of Psychoanalytic Training. *J. Amer. Psychoanal. Assn.*, *58,* 891-925.

Varvin, S. *(*2003*). Which patients* should avoid psychoanalysis*, and which* professionals should avoid psychoanalytic training? *Scandinavian Psychoanalytic Review, 26, 109-122.*

APPENDIX 1

Comparison of Selected Scales

1. Starting point: “Training analysis satisfaction scale” *Analyst feedback questionnaire*. Is there correlation with

1.1 “supervision satisfaction” *Columbia questionnaire*
$r = -0,163$ $p > 0,05$ *no correlation*

1.2 “attachment to – depending on training analyst” *Analyst feedback questionnaire*
$r = 0,765$ $p < 0,001$ *Strong correlation*

1.3 “analytic autonomy and receptive attitude” *Competency questionnaire*
$r = -0,088$ $p > 0,05$ *no correlation*

1.4 “competency level – analytic strength” *Competency questionnaire*
$r = -0,114$ $p > 0,05$ *no correlation*

1.5 “creativity” *Competency questionnaire*
$r = -0,036$ $p > 0,05$ *no correlation*

1.6 From analytic experience questionnaire (yes/no questions):

- number 175, “Have you had the wish/need for another analysis after terminating your analysis?” Contingency coefficient 0,588 $p > 0,05$ *no correlation*
- number 178 “Do you plan to have another analysis?” (Contingency coefficient 0,61 $p > 0,05$ *no correlation*

2. Starting point: “competency level – analytic strength” *Competency questionnaire*. Is there correlation with

2.1 “creativity” *Competency questionnaire*
$r = 0,894$ $p < 0,001$ *strong correlation*

2.2 “strategic analytic knowledge” *Competency questionnaire*
$r = 0,911$ $p < 0,001$ *strong correlation*

2.3 "analytic autonomy and receptive attitude" *Competency questionnaire*
r = 0,966 p<0,001 strong correlation

The strong correlation is influenced by the fact that some items are shared by the scales. However that does not explain the correlations; still, the result has to be interpreted cautiously.

3. Starting point: "creativity." *Competency* Is there correlation with

3.1 "positive alliance scale" *Analyst feed-back questionnaire*
r=0,075 p>0,05 no correlation

3.2 "negative alliance scale" *Analyst feed-back questionnaire*
r=-0,197 p>0,05 no correlation

3.3 "positive personality quality scale" *Analyst feed-back questionnaire*
r=-0,003 p>0,05 no correlation

3.4 "analytic autonomy and receptive attitude" *Competency questionnaire*
r = 0,906 p<0,001 strong correlation

4. Starting point: "openness in supervision" *Columbia questionnaire.*

4.1 "satisfaction in supervision" *Columbia questionnaire*
r = 0,733 p<0,001strong correlation

4.2 "satisfaction with training analysis" *Analyst feedback questionnaire*
r=-0,04 p>0,05 no correlation

APPENDIX 2

Guidelines: "Recently Qualified Young Analysts Interview (PIEE)"

I. The Working Hypothesis

Our working hypothesis is that the process of interview may stir up several anxieties in the participants, e.g., worries about confidentiality and/or fears not to be understood, etc. that can restrict their degree of openness. This requires special relational attitude from the side of the interviewer as well as to make clear in the beginning that there are special procedures which ensure confidentiality.

II. Topics Related to Structure of the Interview

Prior to the Interview

Every interviewer must contact the participants he is responsible to interview via e-mail or/and skype. This contact is important for putting the interviewer – interviewee pair into personal relationship by presenting each other and initiating some kind of exchange. It is advisable the interviewer to present the aims of the interview, its duration, to answer questions and to reach agreement on the time schedule.

Beginning of the Interview

It is important every interview to begin with introduction. We recommend the following one:

> "Now I am interested in how you experience your process of acquiring psychoanalytic competence during your training. I am curious about all sorts of elements that you connect to this process. Feel free to elaborate whenever you want. It is not of primary importance that you answer my questions, I am first and foremost interested in what you emphasize in your learning process."

The End of the Interview

Because we are interested from as much transference data as possible we invite the interviewees to offer their reflections concerning the interview interaction and their relationship to the interviewer. We suggest inviting the interviewees to turn their attention on how they experience the process of interview itself. Possible questions are: *"Looking back, you may have some reflections concerning how you experienced this interview and my way of interviewing you?; "You may for example feel insecure concerning how I will secure your confidentiality towards others in the research group?; You have described experiences and processes, which may give you a feeling of vulnerability in relation to how we in the research team will interpret the data?; You have been describing your training experience in a foreign language; in what degree do you find that it has distorted or restricted your ability to describe this process with "good enough" precision."*

Concerning the articulation of the proposed introductory sentences and the questions in the interview guide, we need to practice. It is highly probable that otherwise the interviewees will experience us to sound clumsy and not authentic.

After the Interview

In order to analyze possible non-verbal processes and transferences in the interview relationship in an object-relational perspective, after the end of the interview we should write down our reflections concerning the quality of the interview interaction.

The Duration of the Interview

Due to understanding that the in-depth reflections on the training process is hugely complex and difficult task, we advise the interview to take between 2 and 3 hours. It is supposed the interviewer to manage the time frame in such a way to ensure maximum rich and precise verbal and nonverbal data.

The Language of Interview

It is very probable that some of the interviewees can have problems in describing their experience in foreign language. It is advisable if you sense that the interviewee is struggling with expressing something, to tell him /her to try put it in other words in order to make sure you get it right.

III. The Content of the Interview

While exploring the topic "Motivation to become a psychoanalyst", we advise to ask "why" instead "how" the interviewee became an analyst. The why-question is more challenging then "how" as it addresses our motivation with an especially in-depth focus related to possible influences of the interviewee's personal past on their interest to became psychoanalysts.

IV. The Form of the Interview

The Attitude of the Interviewer

Degree of projection: An important question is how much projective space we should create in the interview and also what sort of comments the interviewer preferably should make use of? The answer to this question depends on which kind of data we want and which kind of analysis we will do. We want to obtain both verbal and non-verbal data, so our primary aim must be to stimulate the interviewees to speak as well as to be careful about pauses, mistakes and the use of "uh, hm", etc.

The order of focal points vs the flow of associations. The decision to ensure as much projective space as possible (e.g Strømme, Gullestad, Stänicke, & Killingmo, 2010) influences the attitude of the interviewer. For example, the general guideline is to follow the interview guide, but in cases when the interviewee elaborates the issues earlier then the order of focal points or he/she jumps from topic to topic we suggest to follow the interviewee. This means we are more interested from the flow of the associations and natural course of the interview.

Further reflections: After the interviewee has elaborated more freely on every focal point and he/she seems to have finished, we suggest that the interviewer asks if the interviewee wants to add something more. Another formulation could be: "I think/feel that I have understood your elaboration and there seems not to be any element that is difficult for me to understand, so I suggest that we continue."

Interviewers' intervention. The forms of the comments of the interviewers may preferably be questions, affirmations (e.g., Killingmo, 1995, 2006) and mirroring. We do not support to use tentative interpretations during the interviews, primarily because this may increase the interviewees' feelings of vulnerability and exposure and also turn the interview too much in the direction of an analytic situation.

The pilot interviews shows that it is possible interviewers to oscillate between listening and having inner reflections about the training process of the interviewee and about what was going on in the interview relationship without being restricted to make comments. It is possible to make pauses in order to think on the material, to make comments and to check if we understand the interviewee correctly. We can ask questions but also to skip topics already explored. Sometime it is possible to make in-depth interpretations or comment on the material, but we do not support that kind of interventions in the interviews.

In: Psychoanalytic Theory
Editors: K. Martin and M. Siegward
ISBN: 978-1-53612-484-2

Chapter 2

FROM SUBLIMATION TO AFFECT INTEGRATION: PSYCHOANALYTIC APPROACHES TO CREATIVITY FROM FREUD TO SELF-PSYCHOLOGY

Zoltan Kovary*[*]*, PhD
Department of Clinical Psychology and Addiction,
Eötvös Loránd University, Budapest, Hungary, EU

ABSTRACT

The psychoanalytic approach to creativity and arts has always been one of the most popular and influential utilizations of depth-psychology. The birth of this concept was connected to Freud's very specific and important relationship with the aesthetic phenomena. Apart from the fact that he was an outstanding writer and that in his publications he cited much more writers than scientists, it was not even incidental that he began to investigate the psychology of artistic creativity. His ideas about

[*] kovary.zoltan@gmail.com.

creativity were based on the theory of sublimation, and studying the creative process he invented an outstanding but much debated research method called psychobiography. During the decades of the 20th century, the psychoanalytic ideas about creativity transformed according to the development of psychoanalytic theory and practice. The most outstanding authors of this research area were ego-psychologist Ernst Kris and British object relations theorists Melanie Klein and Donald Winnicott. In the last decades of the 20th century, different representatives of self-psychology (Heinz Kohut, Daniel Stern, Robert Stolorow & George Atwood) established a new theoretical framework for psychoanalytic creativity research: they broke up with Freud's biologism and concentrated on the importance of personal and intersubjective affective experiences. In this chapter, I will present these historical-theoretical changes, but I will focus on two other important topics as well. One of them is the question of illness and health in the creative process, while the other is the influence of psychoanalytic creativity theory on other psychological trends like neo-analytic schools, existential psychology or transpersonal psychology.

Keywords: psychoanalysis, Freud, creativity, sublimation, psychobiography, ego psychology, object relations theories, self-psychology, madness

INTRODUCTION

Although Carl Rogers (1959) declared that creativity is a key question concerning the future of mankind, this topic became popular among researchers only after World War II (Anderson, 1959). This is strange, because from the age of Romanticism we have to talk about the cult of creativity (Doorman, 2006), and from that era - beside romantic love - creative activity became one of the most important dimensions of self-fulfillment for humans (Baumeister, 1987). Nevertheless, it does not mean that in the first part of the 20th Century psychologists totally ignored this topic: the two most important trends that were interested in these kinds of questions were Gestalt-psychology and psychoanalysis. Psychoanalysts and Gestalt-psychologists established the two basic approaches to the psychology of creativity: cognitive and personality psychological perspectives (Hilgard, 1959). Gestalt-psychologists like Max Wertheimer

(1938) studied the aspects of productive thinking, while Freud defined the most important features of the artist's character (Freud, 1963/1916-17). In the first ever written psychobiography about Leonardo da Vinci (Freud, 1957/1910) Freud analyzed the interrelations between the artist's personality, life history and creative activity.

In the following chapter, I will try to unfold the evolution of the psychoanalytic perspective on creativity from the beginning until the end of the 20th Century. First, I am going to take a brief look at some historical antecedents: the ancient Greeks (Plato, Aristotle), the representatives of *Lebensphilosophie* (Schopenhauer, Nietzsche) and some ideas of 19th Century natural scientific reductionism. After that, I will examine how the development of Freud's own scientific creativity determined his turning to the question of arts at a certain point of his career. Following this, I will present the concerning ideas of the different schools of psychoanalysis (ego-psychology, object relations theories, self-psychology, etc.), but I am also going to mention some other trends in personality psychology (neo-analytic approaches, existential psychologies, transpersonal psychology, etc.) that were also deeply influenced by Freud's dynamic approach to this topic. At the end of the chapter, I will examine the role of illness and health in creativity that has been an important issue during the century long development of this discourse.

The Historical Antecedents of Psychoanalytic Theory on Creativity

In the history of arts there had been three important periods when the significance of the artist's personality became more and more important: the ages of the ancient Greeks and Reneissance (Wittkower & Wittkower, 1963) and in the era of Romanticism (Safranski, 2014). Some artists and philosophers of these ages strongly influenced Sigmund Freud's view on artistic creation. As he was a highly cultured, well-read person interested not only in hard sciences, Freud was experienced in literature, mythology, archaeology and fine arts as well (Jones, 1953-57). These inspirations prevailed directly, when for example he used mythological motifs like the Oedipal myth or the myth of Narcissus in order to give name to his psychological discoveries. It is also notable that the first version of his psychotherapy method was named "cathartic" after Aristotle's theory on aesthetic effects (Sulloway, 1979). Beside Sophocles the most important antique author Freud cited was Plato. Freud (1961/1925) claimed that the psychoanalytic meaning of sexuality was something similar that Plato explicated as 'Eros' in "Symposium". In Plato's works we can find several ideas that are similar to some psychoanalytic concepts, for example about dreams or the structure of the soul (Durant, 1926). But what is more important in here that in "Phaidros" (2002) Plato unfolded his ideas about artistic inspiration, and according to these thoughts inspiration requires altered states of mind that he called "divine madness" or mania. What we see here is a source of the famous "madness and genius" narrative about eminent creativity that influenced the forthcoming centuries including psychoanalysis. Plato's disciple Aristotle – following the medical ideas of Hippocrates - linked eminent creativity to melancholia, while in the 15th Century Italian Neoplatonist Marsilio Ficino regarded mania and melancholia as the two sides of the same coin (Wittkower & Wittkower, 1964).

The direct antecedents of Freudian creativity theory can be found in 19th Century Romanticism; Lionel Trilling (1963) pronouncedly emphasized that Freud intellectually fulfilled its ideas. The age of Romanticism established the cult of the self, the cult of creativity and music, the cults of freedom, passions, imagination, dream, madness/illness, love-death, night and darkness (Safranski, 2014), and also invented the idea of the unconscious (Koestler, 1964). These topics are all there in Freud's psychoanalytic writings. The artist in Romanticism became the symbol of freedom and authenticity, who is expressing personal emotional experiences in his/her works, and as a genius s/he has the ability to cross the boundaries of consciousness in order to be inspired and gain divine knowledge about human existence. These boundary challenging experiences, visiting the "other side" and the relentless fight for independence are not safe activities: the artist often has to face isolation, poverty, illness, madness, addiction and early death in exchange of the rebellion against conventions and repressive power.

The artists and thinkers of Romanticism advanced several psychoanalytic ideas concerning arts and the unconscious. In "The Act of Creation" Arthur Koestler (1964) demonstrated how the idea of the unconscious evolved from Georg Lichtenberg and Goethe to Carl Gustav Carus and Eduard von Hartmann in the 19th Century. In his book on Goethe and Beethoven Romain Rolland (1931) wrote about the importance of "musical unconscious", as music occupied the highest place in the Romantic hierarchy of arts. In this context we have to mention composer Richard Wagner. Wagner's life and works seem to be a quintessence of Romanticism, and some of his ideas advanced Freudian psychology (Paneth, 1985). Wagner was the first who discovered that mythological motifs are not fairy tales: they represent general psychological truth concerning human situations. He also placed love and eroticism in the focus of his musical dramas (Magee, 2001). Thomas Mann (1965) described Wagner's art with the following formula: mythology plus music plus psychology, while Friedrich Nietzsche wrote that "the prelude to *Lohengrin* gives the first, overly insidious, overly successful example of how to hypnotize with music" (Nietzsche, 2005/1888, p. 246).

The most important (late) Romantic influences on Freud's creativity theory were two philosophers who were both connected to Wagner in a way: Nietzsche and Schopenhauer. Wagner was a follower and admirer of Arthur Schopenhauer's philosophy and aesthetic ideas concerning the metaphysical importance of music (Schopenhauer, 1966/1818-19). In his "Autobiographical Study" Freud (1964/1925) acknowledged some parallels between psychoanalysis and the philosophy of Schopenhauer, but he stated that he read the philosopher's works only after his own discoveries so there hadn't been any direct influences. Schopenhauer (ibid.) attributed similar "self-healing" functions to aesthetic experiences as Freud did in "Civilization and its Discontents" (1961/1930); but the philosopher's ideas about the necessary "somnambulism" of the brilliant artists and other thoughts are also regarded as advances of some psychoanalytic concepts (Mann, 1936).

The Wagner-admirer-then-hater Nietzsche's influence is more complicated. Although there are a lot of similarities between the theories of Nietzsche and Freud on personality, dreams, illness, arts, morals or religion (Assoun, 2000), the nature of this relationship has never been clarified satisfactorily. Freud (1964/1925) acknowledged some surprising similarities, but he denied the direct influences heavily. These similarities are rather striking in the realm of art-psychology. Nietzsche, two decades before Freud, used psychological concepts like "hypnosis", "hysteria" or "neurosis" in his explanations about the artist, and he also stated the following: "One must examine the artist himself, and his psychology (critique of the drive to play as a release of force, a pleasure in change, in impressing one's soul on something foreign, the absolute egoism of the artist, etc.) What drives he sublimates." (Nietzsche, 1968/1889, p. 359).

In this paragraph Nietzsche literally advanced Freud's theory about sublimation. We might never learn if Freud's analogous theory was based on direct reception or not, but these similarities have their life historical/cultural/contexts that are easier to unfold. Nietzsche and Freud both had their own Oedipal stories of their dead, lost father (Rudnytsky, 1987). As scholars they are both representing the naturalist-vitalist perspective of man, trying to find one simple instinct (power, sexuality) behind human complexity (Scheler, 1962/1928). They developed their philosophical/psychological theories about the artist by analyzing a single person that they were influenced by and identified with. Nietzsche interpreted Wagner, while Freud investigated Leonardo; both psychological/psychobiographical studies included indirect self-analyzes (Kőváry, 2011; 2016). And finally, as Stephen Jay Gould wrote: "almost all major ideas arise more than once independently and often virtually at the same time – and thus that great scientists are embedded in their culture, not divorced from them. Most great ideas are 'in the air' and several scholars simultaneously wave their nets" (Gould, 1980, pp. 47-48).

FREUD, ARTS AND CREATIVITY

Sigmund Freud had a very special relationship with arts, especially with literature. He was honored with Goethe-prize in 1930 although this was usually given to writers and not scientists (Schivelbusch, 1994). In his works he cited much more writers (Shakespeare, Goethe, Schiller, Heine) than scientists. He acknowledged that psychoanalytic case studies can be read like short stories (Freud, 1955/1893-95), and also declared that writers are always one step ahead of scientists concerning psychological discoveries (Freud, 1959/1906). He tended to test his new psychological theories in art-psychological articles before publishing a more "serious" theoretical writing about them (Hertz, 1979). When he got involved in writing his essay about Leonardo, it became the most important thing for him for several months and he felt an urge to publish it as soon as it was possible (Elms, 1994). According to Hans-Martin Lohmann's interpretation, Freud's oeuvre began with a collection of short stories ("Studies on Hysteria") and ended with a historical novel ("Moses and Monotheism") (Lohmann, 2008).

It was not accidental that Freud began to deal with the problems of arts and creativity, and his theories on artistic creation were not accessory compared to his more "serious" concepts about psychopatholgical phenomena and psychotherapy. The intellectual road that led him to this topic was related to the development of his own creativity, including not only scientific but artistic elements as well that he successfully subordinated to scientific aims[1]. If we take a look at his creative products (like writings about psychopathology, psychotherapy, dreams, parapraxes, jokes, arts, anthropological questions, religion, group phenomena, etc.), at first glance this activity might seem unreasonably diverse. But if we investigate the development of his creative activity historically, we will find a "network of enterprises" (Gruber, H. E., Bödecker, K. & Wallace,

[1] These efforts are not always successful in an outstanding person's life: in the Leonardo-essay Freud emphasized that Leonardo's scientific interest inhibited then totally suppressed the artistic side.

D. 2005); one can perceive how his investigations evolved systematically as he discovered the languages of the unconscious one after the other.

Freud started his discoveries with the study of psychopathological phenomena, especially hysteria in his private practice. He wanted to become a researcher physician, but because of his Jewish origins he did not have a chance to build a career at universities at that time. His boss, Ernst Brücke suggested him to start a private practice; so it became the field of his investigations and discoveries (Jones, 1953-57). In the 1890's Freud (first with the help of Josef Breuer, then alone) discovered that neurotic symptoms are the expressions of repressed unconscious desires and intentions (Freud, 1959/1893-95). During this time, as Freud's patients began to talk about their dreams while doing free associations, he realized that dreams[2] had the same structure as neuroses; the way the unconscious transforms latent contents into manifest forms ("dream-work") is absolutely the same as we can see in symptom formation (Freud, 1953/1900). So after the proto-language of the body in hysteria, visual language came into view in dreams. As dreaming is an everyday normal phenomenon, by this step Freud was able to convert clinical knowledge to normal psychology. His intention was namely to create a universal theory about mind which was not limited to the realm of psychopathology (Sulloway, 1979). While dealing with symptoms and dreams in therapies, he also discovered that slips of the tongue and other parapraxes are also organized the same way; so in 1901, in "Psychopatology of Everyday Life" presented the analysis of everyday conduct and verbal products (Freud, 1960/1901). Dreams and slips of the tongue are like bad jokes sometimes, so he started to study humor, and in 1905 he published "Jokes and Their Relation to the Unconscious" (Freud, 1960/1905). In this book he completely focused on verbal activity, defining "joke-work" as something similar to dream-work. The characteristics of jokes made Freud realize, that the formal aspects of psychological formations are equally as important as the content: if we change the linguistic form of the joke, the

[2] Freud had been interested in dreams since his university years, but it was his therapeutic activity that helped him in understanding them (Sulloway, 1979).

emotional impact can fail. Humor is causing catharsis, and it is one of the main tools of aesthetic effect in arts, so the next evident step was the study of artistic products, first of all literature. Freud himself was aware of the fact, that his book on jokes was the first psychoanalytic contribution to the investigation of aesthetic phenomena (Freud, 1957/1914). Two years later, in "Dreams and Delusions in Jensen's Gradiva" (Freud, 1959/1906) Freud began to investigate artistic creativity directly. As dreams in a novel can be interpreted the same way as in everyday life, it seems that the writer is doing the same thing as the psychoanalyst: s/he explores and unfolds the realm of the unconscious. But where is this knowledge about the unconscious coming from in the case of the writer? What are the main psychological tools of transforming the unconscious contents into works of art?

One year later, in "Creative Writers and Day Dreaming" (Freud, 1959/1908) Freud expounded that the psychological source of the artist's creative activity is unconscious fantasy; the region of the psyche that is not limited by reality principle. Fantasies are activated when an everyday experience influences the artist. As he explained: "A strong experience in the present awakens in the creative writer a memory of an earlier experience (usually belonging to his childhood) from which there now proceeds a wish which finds its fulfillment in the creative work. The work itself exhibits elements of the recent provoking occasion as well as of the old memory" (Freud, 1959/1908, p. 151). This structure is similar to the formation of dreams, when day residues ("strong experiences" and their relation to the "actually unconscious") are merging with "old memories" (the "infantile" unconscious) transformed by primary processes like condensation, replacement or symbolization. These similarities show that unconscious fantasies are the common sources of neuroses, dreams and creative products.

In the next two years Freud widened the focus of his art-psychological researches, completed his theory about creativity, and elaborated a research method that made him able to study eminent creativity. In 1910 he finally published his debated "Leonardo da Vinci and a Memory of His Childhood" (Freud, 1957/1910); this is the most important text of classic psychoanalytic art-psychology. The essay is the first complete psychological analysis of artistic creativity, in which Freud applied the entire theoretical arsenal of psychoanalysis, but also introduced some new and significant ideas like narcissism or the importance of primary (maternal) object relations (Blum, 2001). Freud also introduced a new research method called psychobiography, which was different from pathographies that were carried out by psychiatrists at the end of the 19th and the beginning of the 20th Centuries (Kőváry, 2011). Psychobiography is the psychological investigation of a significant person's (artist, scientist) life history and life- work in order to construct a coherent narrative that explains the interrelations between experiences, personality, life historical events and creative products (McAdams, 1988). Although psychobiography has been always debated over its century long history, in the end of the 20th and the beginning of the 21st century – owing to the success of narrative psychology – it gained recognition again (Schultz, 2005; Kőváry, 2011). After "Leonardo" Freud wrote some other important articles in this field - like "The Moses of Michelangelo" (1955/1914), "The Uncanny" (1955/1919) or "Dostoevsky and Parricide" (1961/1928), the complexity and significance of these writings do not come close to the Leonardo-essay.

Freud expounded his ideas about the artist's personality and the dynamics of the creative process very clearly and focused in the 23rd lecture of "Introduction to Psychoanalysis" (Freud, 1963/1916-17). The artist, claims Freud, has intensive instinctual desires; but these wishes do not belong to the adult person's real life personality but to the realm of infantile sexuality, namely partial instincts. As the satisfaction of these infantile instinctual wishes (like sexual curiosity, oral omnipotence, exhibitionism, sadism and masochism, etc.) always have to face obstacles in everyday life, the libido takes its direction towards the inner world, intensifying the "cathexis" of unconscious fantasies. The artist is introverted, but it's not a personality type as in Jung's theory; it refers to the orientation of the libido, the tendency to deal with fantasies in an enhanced manner. Psychological defences like repression are looser in the case of the artist, so these intensified fantasies can enter consciousness more easily; and they are being seen more as challenges instead of threats by the creator. The final important characteristic of the artist is the ability to sublimate these instinctual desires represented in fantasies. Sublimation means transformation of the unconscious material (mostly as disguise and symbolization), and as compromise formations it makes wish- fulfillment possible both for the artist and the recipient of the creative product. Dreams and neurotic symptoms are also compromise formations; the most important difference is that the artist can communicate with the external world successfully by linking transformed fantasies to the shared structures of reality (language, for example).

So sublimation is the central idea of Freud's creativity-theory. But what did he exactly mean by this phrase? If we are not focusing on his metapsychological speculations about sublimation that he presented in for example in "Instincts and Their Vicissitudes" (1957/1915), according to the above mentioned 23rd lecture of "Introduction to Psychoanalysis" (Freud, 1963/1916-17) we can identify three tangible components of this ability. First: the artist knows how to work through day-dreams (or fantasies) in order to make them loose what is too personal, so others can enjoy them too. Second: s/he understands how to tone them down so they "do not easily betray their origin from proscribed sources" (p. 377). Here Freud refers to sexual, aggressive or narcissistic contents that can be enjoyed only in censored or transformed ways. Wish fulfillment in creating and enjoying works of art is similar to that of dreaming, as dreams are the prototypes of disguised wish-fulfillment. But I would like to add that this process is not only about enjoyment; the sources can be traumatic in dreams and in creation either. Talking about the latter the artistic tools that establish an "optimal aesthetic distance" (Scheff, 1979) psychologically help the artist to bear the effects of traumas. This process is partly based on "primary processes" that Freud identified as the essential forms of dream-work[3] (condensation, replacement, symbolization). If dream-work is not

[3] It is notable, that - following Jacques Lacan -Terry Eagleton (1983) called these primary processes of dream-work primarily poetical, because condensation fits to forming metaphors, while replacement equals with the use of metonymy. Nietzsche was also aware

successful, so during the construction of a particular dream it cannot establish an "aesthetic distance", cannot hide the origins of the fantasy, the dreamer experience anxiety and s/he wakes up. In arts if a wounded, traumatized artist (for example a Holocaust survivor) gets too close to his/her original trauma by decreasing the optimal aesthetic distance for example moving away from heterobiographies to autobiography, it might cause fatal re-traumatization (Rosenblum, 2012).

The third component is the artist's "mysterious power of shaping some particular material until it has become a faithful image of his fantasy" (Freud, 1963/1916-17, p. 377). How can we evaluate this aspect? As I referred to it above, in his book on jokes Freud (1960/1905) realized that beside the special and necessary drive-contents (sexuality, aggression) the way of shaping these contents also contributes the cathartic impact of the joke. Later he also acknowledged that "poetic treatment is impossible without softening and disguise" (Freud, 1961/1923, p. 188). But how can an artist achieve that? How can s/he use words so successfully that will make the enjoyment of these contents possible? This is the question of giftedness; and Freud declared that psychoanalysis "can do nothing towards elucidating the nature of artistic gift, nor can it explain the means by the artist works – artistic technique" (Freud, 1950/1925, pp. 119-120).

In spite of this five years after this declaration Hungarian psychoanalyst Imre Hermann (2007/1930) constructed a complex psychoanalytic model of talent in which he improved Freud's original theory. He claimed that talent have three components: (1) talent as a whole, which is a latent bio-psychological potential, (2) inducing (external) forces like emergence of a new libido object or experiencing a trauma, and (3) motivational drive-factors like Freudian partial instincts (oral, anal, phallic). Most of the time talent emerges under the influence of inducing forces, but its maintenance depends on the motivational effects of partial instincts. Hermann emphasized that the partial "oral" instinct is only a component of a more complex system, the "hand-eye-mouth system" that

of this, as he wrote: "In dreaming we use up too much of our artistic capacity - and therefore often have too little of it during the day" (1986/1878-1880, p. 358).

is an aspect of the so called "clinging instinct" or "clinging syndrome". Just because this system is evolving within the context of a dual union with the mother (Hermann, 1984/1943), this concept refers to the same phenomenon as John Bowlby's attachment-theory decades later. Hermann (2007/1930) argued that eyes or hands are serving as erogenous zones the same way as mouth; the hypercathexis of these zones can be specific for examples in the cases of painters (Resnik, 2000; Kőváry, 2009). Hermann was also a pioneer in creativity research; he was the first psychoanalyst who studied the psychology of natural scientists: in the 1920's he systematically investigated scientists like Darwin, Fechner or outstanding Hungarian mathematician János Bolyai with the use of psychobiography (Hermann, 2013)[4].

The Contribution of Ego-Psychology

Ego psychology improved Freud's structural theory on personality focusing on the ego: how its functions contribute the process of adaptation (Fonagy & Target, 2003). It had different schools, for example the British (Anna Freud) and the US variants (Heinz Hartmann), which later evolved on as developmental ego-psyhology (Edith Jacobson, Margaret Mahler) (Mitchell & Black, 1996). The growing popularity of ego-psychology – especially in America – influenced creativity research heavily in the middle of the 20th Century. As Noy (1979) emphasized that from this time analysts – instead of interpreting the latent, unconscious content of the products - began to concentrate on the psychological mechanisms of expression, the structure of the creative personality and the ways of forming a "good shape". In this subchapter I will discuss the ego-psychological reinterpretation of sublimation, the way ego-psychologists conceptualized the role of personality structures and mental processes in

[4] It is notable, that mainstream academic psychology began to deal with the psychological background of sciences only in the 21st Century. See Gorman & Feist (Eds.), 2013.

creativity, and finally I will refer to the most important ego-psychological creativity theory elaborated by Ernst Kris.

Outstanding authors of ego-psychology like Heinz Hartmann (1955), Ernst Kris (1955) or Joseph Sandler and W. G. Joffe (1966) intended to clarify the role of sublimation in personality dynamics including creativity. But in my opinion these theoretical speculations are mostly focusing on the supposed metapsychological background, and therefore they do not contribute the psychoanalytic understanding of creativity as much as Hans Loewald's ideas at that time. Loewald was not ego-psychologist in the strict sense of the word; he also supported classic psychoanalysis, object relations theories and self-psychology. In his book "Sublimation" (1988)– instead of following Hartmann's formalism and metapsychological speculations about the vicissitudes of libido and aggression - he layed stress on the mother-infant matrix and the development of the ego in this context, claiming that "sublimation is passion transformed" (p. 9). According to Loewald the development of the ego is based on the differentiation of the self and the object, while this passion is an internalized motivation, a wish for reconciliation. This process is not a form of defense, but an important progressive process guarded by defense mechanisms. Reconciliation is about the restoration of the lost unity by using symbols, for example words. In order to achieve this, one needs a special way of verbalization, a "poetic language", in which primary process aspects (based on pleasure principle) are in balance with the secondary process aspects (based on reality principle). It means that fantasy and reality pervade each other (Loewald, 1980).

This latter is connected to the role of personality structures and mental processes in the creative process. Ego psychologists believe that the different structures of personality and the mental processes that they are dominated by have different functions in the creative process. Lawrence Kubie (1958) emphasized that the success of the artistic performance depends on the flexibility of the preconscious; it mediates between the relentless wish-fulfillment of the unconscious and the also relentless censorship of the conscious mind. Ehrenzweig (1962) and Martindale (1978) were both talking about the engagement of primary processes (concrete thinking, irrationality, autistic disposition) and secondary processes (abstract thinking, logic, reality orientation) during creation. Martindale supposed that they form a continuum, while Arieti (1964) assumed that there are "tertiary processes" as well to synchronize these different forms of functioning. Robert Klein (1971) presumed that as these primary process characteristics are also present in psychopathological phenomena, so we have to suppose a continuum of psychotic and creative functioning. On the psychotic pole we can find intensive primary process functioning, decreased secondary process functioning and reduced capacity to synthesize contents, while on the creative pole both primary and secondary process activities and capacity to synthesize are intensified. According to David Beres (1957) the ego can reduce an entire creative subsystem that is able to take over the role of the whole personality and can compensate psychological deficits.

The most important creativity theory within this trend belongs to Ernst Kris, who was a psychoanalyst and an art historian at the same time contributing psychoanalytic art-psychology in many ways. His most important concept in this field is a model about the creative process called "regression in the service of the ego" (Kris, 2000/1952). According to this the creative process is divided into two parts: inspiration and elaboration[5]. Inspiration is a well-known dimension of creating for ages. As I mentioned above, in Romanticism artists developed different techniques to cross the boundaries of the conscious self in order to be inspired by extreme aesthetic and emotional experiences. From a psychoanalytic perspective this psychological condition is called regression, because during this period the personality is temporarily dominated by the unconscious and primary processes. The boundaries of the conscious and the unconscious are becoming permeable, and - according to introjective and projective mechanisms - the person tends to identify the stimulating impulses to create as something external. The elaboration phase is dominated by

[5] Salvador Dalí called his method of creating "paranoiac-critical method" which refers to two phases, one "mad" and one "sane", that is similar to Kris' idea (Kővváry, 2009).

secondary processes[6], but beside this another dimensions come into view like evaluation of the work by identification with the audience. According to Kris the creative process has id, superego and ego aspects. It is always connected with wish-fulfillment (id), but scientific and artistic discoveries are always about breaking conventional rules (superego), and – in contrast with dreaming or psychopathological phenomena – this process is serving the goals of the ego; regression is temporary, and the standards of the ego functions are not falling back on a primitive level.

OBJECT RELATIONS THEORIES AND CREATIVITY

Object relations theories were the most influential trends in post-Freudian psychoanalysis in the second part of the 20th Century. Influenced by Freud's basic works like "Mourning and Melancholia" (1957/1917) or "Inhibitions, Symptoms and Anxiety" (1959/1926)[7] and the heritage of the Budapest School of Psychoanalysis led by Sándor Ferenczi (Aron & Harris, 1993), object relations theories moved away psychoanalysis from "one-man psychology" towards relational perspectives. Ferenczi is said to be a founder of modern psychoanalysis according to his radical interpersonal approach, his view on traumas, countertransference and the psychoanalytic process. He was the training analyst of outstanding British object relations theorists like Melanie Klein and Michael Bálint, and eminent American interpersonal analyst Clara Thompson (Székács-Weisz & Keve, 2012), but he also influenced Donald Winnicott (Tonnesmann, 2012) and Erich Fromm (Bocciagaluppi, 1993).

---

[6] It is very interesting that while scientists tend to lay stress on irrational, inspirational phase when they are talking about their discoveries, some artists tend to emphasize the importance of logical thinking in creating (Koestler, 1964). This might be a compensation, because people tend to think of scientists as "cool headed" and of artists as "hot headed".

[7] It is remarkable, that the first Freudian paper that indirectly introduced the perspective of early object relations was the Leonardo-essay, the essence of Freud's creativity theory (Blum, 2001).

Object relation theories enriched psychoanalytic approach to creativity in many ways. (1) Authors highlighted that the origins of the self are relational and not individual, so its functions and formations – like creativity - always contain relational aspects. (2) Classic psychoanalysis (and ego-psychology) related creativity to the sublimation of libidinal wishes and partial instincts and saw it as the continuation and substitution of infantile playing and enjoyment. With the idea of depressive position and reparation Melanie Klein and her followers emphasized the importance of aggressive feelings and guilt towards the object, and they believed that creativity plays a central role in overcoming depressive position (Segal, 1988/1964). (3) Creativity is also a basic concept in Winnicott's developmental theory; with his idea of "primary creativity" Winnicott (1971) extracted creativity from clinical context. (4) By focusing on the internalization and externalization of relational experiences, object relational authors clarified the differences between introjection, identification, projection and self-objectivation (Hamilton, 1999), that determine the psychodynamics of the creative process. In this subchapter I will concentrate on Klein's and Winnicott's theories, because - beside Freud and Kris - they were the most important contributors of this research area in the 20th Century.

Melanie Klein's theory on creativity is an integral part of her view about early personality development (Klein, 1930; Segal, 1988/1964). Klein supposed there are two "positions" in early personality development: paranoid-schizoid and depressive. Positions are not phases but modes of handling psychological experiences, especially libidinal and aggressive drives, containing special forms of object relations, anxieties and defences. In paranoid-schizoid position the representation of the self and the object are only partially differentiated and split (they are entirely good or bad). Good and bad experiences (based on libidinal and aggressive impulses) are linked to the introjected and projected parts of the object; anxiety has paranoid characteristics, and primitive defense mechanisms (splitting, projective identification, denial, idealization and devaluation) are trying to defend the introjected good parts of the object and the self from aggression and persecution. These processes are taking part in the unconscious fantasy. After the infant has internalized enough good experiences to construct the solid internal representation of the good object that s/he can identify with, the integration of the good and bad parts of the self and the object come into view. In depressive position representations are no more split (the beginning of ambivalence!), anxieties are becoming depressive (fear of separation, feelings of remorse and guilt because of the aggressive attacks on the object in fantasy). Defences are more mature in this position (repression, reaction formation), and reality orientation is starting to dominate over fantasies. The child/the person[8] is feeling an urge to restore/recreate the destroyed/lost object, which process is based on symbol using. Symbol using requires to make difference between the internal world and external reality (because the symbol is representing the object and they are not one and the same), which means that the individual has to give up his/her claim to have omnipotent control over the object. From psychodynamic perspective this latter aspect it is connected to grief, so the creative restoration of the lost/destroyed object in depressive fantasies[9] and in activity means that the sublimation of impulses, the reparation of the lost/destroyed object and the psychological work of mourning are strongly tied together. Klein's French follower, Janine Chasseguet-Smirgel (1984) later declared that creative activity – beside the reparation of the object – contains another important dimension: the restoration of self-integrity[10].

[8] It is important to emphasize that although Klein is talking about the very early period of life, depressive position never comes to an end as we always have to cope with its conflicts in our entire life (Segal, 1988/1964).

[9] Julia Kristeva (1987), the follower of Klein and Lacan also wrote about "the melancholic imaginary", which is derived from the discovery of the "imaginary father". It means that the child realizes that s/he is not the only object of the mother's desires, and constructing fantasies is about looking for this "paradise lost". She also drew up the necessity of symbolic matricide in creativity (Kristeva, 2001). This is about abolishing symbiosis with the mother, because symbolization requires separation, to make difference between the self and the object, fantasy and reality, symbol and symbolized. These ideas were used in a psychobiographical study about two Hungarian cousin-writers a few years ago (Kőváry, 2013).

[10] It is possible that the restoration of the object and the self is sometime sonly partially successful. In the case of traumas, – according to Ferenczi (1949/1932; 2007/1933) - the self is splitting into different parts, and the experiencing part is getting fixed to the trauma, unconsciously repeating it in dreams or illusions. Another parts might develop

Klein influenced Donald Winnicott, who was also very critical about some Kleinian concepts, like the acceptance of death instinct (Winnicott, 1965). Winnicott started a new era in psychoanalytic research on creativity with concepts like "primary creativity" and "transitional phenomena" (Winnicott, 2005/1971). He believed that creativity is not a protection against anxiety or about working thorough conflicts and traumas, but his "theory includes a belief that living creatively is a healthy state, and that compliance is a sick basis for life" (Winnicott, 2005/1971, p. 87). He was against the psychobiographical study of eminent creators, because, as he said, focusing on life historical interrelations in these writings "the main theme is being circumvented, that of the creative impulse itself" (p. 93). In his definition "creative impulse is therefore something that can be looked at as a thing in itself, something that of course is necessary if an artist is to produce a work of art, but also as something that is present when anyone - baby, child, adolescent, adult, old man or woman - looks in a healthy way at anything or does anything deliberately, such as making a mess with faeces or prolonging the act of crying to enjoy a musical sound" (p. 69)[11].

According to Winnicott's theory, creativity is the essential part of early personality (self) development, and it remains the part of healthy functioning lifelong. But how does it emerge during the early years? Winnicott discovered its origins in the so called "transitional phenomena": the experience of transitional space and the use of transitional objects. These phenomena emerge in the context of early object relations. The "good enough mother" during "primary maternal preoccupation" is getting involved in the subjective world (subjective reality, fantasies) of the infant

psychopathological symptoms (regression), while a third part can progress establishing a "creative subsystem" that evolves a kind of a balance. I have tried to demonstrate this version recently in an article about eminent Hungarian painter Tivadar Csontváry Kosztka (1853-1919), whose talent and psychosis both emerged due to a traumatic experience of natural disaster that probably had personal meanings for him (Kőváry, 2012).

[11] I would like to add that in his view Winnicott – similar to humanistic and positive psychologist – does not make a difference between "everyday" and "eminent" creativity, or, in other words, "Big C" and "Little C" (Kaufman & Beghetto, 2009). This is important, because empirical research (for example Richards, 1993) clearly showed that psychopathology always matters in the cases of eminent creativity, but in everyday creativity it is subsidiary. See this chapter's subchapter "Illness, health and creativity".

by establishing a "holding environment". By taking part in the infant's "madness" the mother contributes the infant's illusion of omnipotence; it means that she constructs a psychological world around the infant which is entirely about the wish fulfillment of the infant. But sooner or later the infant has to face objective reality; the world and the object is not under his/her omnipotent control, and wish fulfillment is not unimpeded. If the transition from subjective to objective reality is too drastic (for example the mother is too intrusive and negates the child's subjective world), the child will hide his/her subjective world and develop a "false self" in order to adapt to the expectations of the caregiver(s). To avoid the traumatic experience of ruthless external reality, with the help of the mother the infant has to experience transitional phenomena in a potential space that mediate between external and internal, reality and fantasy, self and object. Transitional space is a realm where the infant - on the way to accept reality - can still experience omnipotence, keeping a special, available object (transitional object) under control. The most important activity that belongs to this realm is playing.

Winnicott emphasized that creativity (just like other cultural activities) is growing in the soil of these transitional phenomena and playing, and in adulthood they take the form of different cultural activities. As he wrote: "We adults use the arts and religion for the off-moments which we all need in the course of reality-testing and reality-acceptance" (Winnicott, 1958, p. 224). Winnicott's creativity theory was highly influential; we can discover these effects in the writings of Marion Milner (1956), Arnold Modell (1970) or Christopher Bollas (1978). Following Winnicott, Bollas constructed a term called "transformational object", which refers to a well-known experience; creating and receiving artistic products can change the conditions of the self (like attunement) by transforming emotions. The first transformational object is the mother, who can change the infant's emotional states by the aesthetic features of her conduct (like the tone of the voice or singing). We internalize these experiences, and in our whole life we are trying to create or find objects (like works of art) that can bring off similar affective changes in ourselves.

SELF-PSYCHOLOGY AND INTERSUBJECTIVITY THEORY

In the 1970's a new version of psychoanalysis emerged in the United States under the name of self-psychology; its leading person was Heinz Kohut. In the beginning self-psychology was regarded as a theory and method to understand and treat people with narcissistic issues, and Kohut himself treated his new approach as a completion of ego-psychology (Kohut, 2009/1971). In the following years Kohut extended his theoretical view, and self-psychology became a new paradigm within psychoanalysis (Kohut, 2014/1977; 2013/1984). Kohut emphasized that psychoanalytic situation is the only real source of analytic knowledge, and it is epistemologically demarcated by the analyst's empathy and the patient's introspection. In order to understand what is going on in this field one has to apply "pure psychology", as Kohut demanded it ever since his first significant paper, "Introspection, Empathy and Psychoanalysis" (1959). Therefore his school became receptive to endeavors that intended to keep depth psychology away from the biologism, reductionism and scientism of classic psychoanalysis and especially ego-psychology (Karterud, 1999). Because of Kohut's untimely death (1981), self-psychology remained unfinished, that led to the emergence of different trends within self-psychology like developmental self-psychology, affect-theory and intersubjectivity theory (Karterud & Monsen, 1999).

Kohut was a Viennese originally, so he was dedicated to European cultural traditions. He was a great fan of music, and it is possible that the insights that led him to drafting self-psychology-theory came from his musical experiences (Dimitrievic, 2013). Throughout his life he dealt with several artistic and other cultural phenomena (Kohut, 1980). In his earlier period (in "The Analysis of the Self", 1971) he viewed creativity as a mature form of narcissism, since he supposed that narcissism is an autonomous developmental line within personality evolving from primitive formations (grandiosity, idealization) to more mature versions (ambitions, following valuable ideals). The primitive forms are regarded as normal in early childhood, and if the caregivers respond to them with empathy, the bipolar self (grandiosity and idealization) will develop into a cohesive self with mature narcissistic needs like creativity or wisdom. If empathy is missing, the primitive, archaic forms subsist providing a basis for narcissistic disorders. Kohut experienced that during the analytic treatment creative impulses can appear, but they remain durable only if there were intensive creative activities during the patient's childhood.

In his later period (in "The Restoration of the Self", 1977) Kohut - in contrast with Freud's "Guilty Man" - expounded his idea of the modern "Tragic Man". The Guilty Man struggled with his/her conscience in order to reach the satisfaction of instinctual desires; but the Tragic Man of our age is fighting for the cohesion of the fragmented self. Modern artists like Picasso, Stravinsky or Kafka anticipated this condition; that is why Kohut referred to "the hypothesis of artistic anticipation" (Kohut, 2014/1977, p. 285). According to him establishing and maintaining the coherence of the self always requires a special relationship with somebody (or later, something), a "self-object" who/that will support the psychological processing of our experiences by providing the so called "self-object functions". The basic forms of these functions are mirroring and the chance to be idolized. In the early periods of life these are related to parents and caregivers, but later other persons and cultural phenomena can also take the role of the "self-object". The developing individual is internalizing the experiences that occur in the self/self-object matrix (the "transmutative internalization" of the self-object experiences), but we need to find self-objects to re-establish and maintain our self-coherence throughout our whole life-span. Kohut's ideas seem to be similar to the theories of Winnicott and Bollas; critics of his works often emphasize the lack of reference to Winnicott in Kohut's writings; but he is also criticized for widening the meaning of self-object overly (Fonagy & Target, 2003). Kohut's ideas strongly influenced modern psychoanalytic approach to arts and creativity. One of his followers, George Hagman (2000) called creative activity a "transmutative externalization", when the artist is re-establishing the self/self-object matrix not by manipulating the self-structure but by producing transformations in the work of art.

Of post-Kohutian movements I would refer to three authors who were influenced by Kohut's endeavors, but they cannot be called selfpsychologists literally. Daniel Stern's (1985) developmental theory is based on the concept called "senses of self", the personal experience of the world and ourselves. His theory contains some important aspects that are related to the questions of arts and creativity. Stern identified "vitality affects" that appear in the very early period of development; they accompany the experience of vital functions as for example "intensity" or "contrast". The experience of vital affects is based on perception, but humans tend to transform these perceptions into emotions. Artists can transform these feelings into "real" perceptions like colors, forms, voices, intensity in time, while the recipient is able to transform these perceptions into affects by the use of "amodal" and "transmodal" perception. The other aesthetic aspect of his work is related to language use. At a certain point of the development the child is starting to use conventional language to encode and share experiences. But the complexity of personal experiences disappear in verbal communication, as verbal expression is only a perspective and not the entire experience. The part of the self that cannot be expressed via language becomes inaccessible causing a gap inside, and in order to re-establish the coherence of the self by filling these gaps one has to enter the realm of aesthetics. "It is little wonder – wrote Stern - we need art so badly to bridge these gaps in ourselves" (Stern, 1998/1985, p. 181). To bridge this gap in order to restore self-coherence – this is the main psychological aim of creative activity.

Intersubjectivist Robert D. Stolorow and his permanent co-worker George Atwood met Kohutian selfpsycholgy on their way to elaborate "post-Cartesian psychoanalysis" aka "phenomenological contextualism" (Stolorow, 2011). They welcomed Kohut's idea about "pure psychology" as they were about to work out an epistemological background for a dynamic subjectivity-theory using phenomenology, hermeneutics, existentialism and structuralism (Atwood & Stolorow, 1984)[12]. Stolorow

[12] Ever since its birth there has been a debate whether psychoanalysis belongs to "human science psychology" or "natural science psychology" (Walsh, Teo & Baydala, 2014). This issue is

and Atwood represent a radical intersubjectivist approach (Stolorow, Atwood & Brandchaft, 1994); they believe that psychological experiences and the "structures of subjectivity" emerge and maintain in intersubjective context during development and therapy, and the Cartesian idea of the "isolated mind" is only a "myth (Stolorow & Atwood, 1992). One of their most important concepts is "affect integration", they refer to a process that is also organized in intersubjective context. Affective experiences (like traumas) have to find their "relational home" during a dialogue with the empathic Other in order to be recognized and integrated by finding its own personal meaning (Stolorow, Brandchaft & Atwood, 1987). What are the consequences of these ideas concerning creativity? Creative activity, especially in artistic creativity is always related to emotional experiences. That is why it's necessary to talk about "emotional creativity", which is partly different from cognitive creativity focusing on problem solving; it's about expressing emotions in a new, successful and authentic way (Averill & Thomas-Knowles, 1991). Most of the time emotional creativity is put into action by using symbolic systems like language. But how does intersubjectivity come into view in this process? The romantic idea of the "lone creator" is probably a version of the "isolated mind"-myth. If we take a look at the life history of eminent artists and scientist, it usually turns out that although they published their works under their own name, their ideas took their form during a constant dialogue with the Other as co-player or counter-player (Isaacson, 2005). In the history of arts we can see that legendary friendships (Goethe and Schiller, Coleridge and Wordsworth, Van Gogh and Gauguin, Verlaine and Rimbaud) always affect the creative process deeply, and without this context it couldn't be understood. The similar phenomenon exists in scientific creativity, for example in the history of psychology. If we study the relationship of Freud and Ferenczi (Erős, 2004), Jung and Sabina Spielrein (Kőváry, 2015) or

still actual; authors like Stolorow and Atwood vote for human sciences, while others like Gedo (1999) or Fónagy & Target (2003) would link psychoanalysis to natural and neurosciences. Fónagy and Target for example explicitly welcomed American psychoanalyst Otto Kernberg's endeavor to move psychoanalysis from hermeneutic to empirical perspective.

Henry Murray and Christiana Morgan (Kőváry, 2018), we will come to the conclusion that Freud'd, Jung's or Murray's theories on personality wouldn't exist the way we know them if a deep emotional relationship with their co-players hadn't been existed. Co-players can turn into counterplayers without losing their significant influence for example like Wagner in the case of Nietzsche (Kőváry, 2016) or Freud in the case of Jung (Kőváry, 2015).

The idea of intersubjectivity in creativity has an important historical antecedent. In psychology it was the above mentioned Henry Murray who first defined the so called "dyadic creativity: "The psyche is a region – he wrote - where creations may or may not flourish, and if two people are involved, these two regions and their intercommunicating process to be considered… [so we have to talk about] dyadic, rather than monadic creativity. This means that we shall be dealing with two interdependent regions of imagination operating as a single system" (Murray, 1959, pp. 109-110). It is important to mention that Stolorow and Atwood are both connected to Murray's personological tradition. Stolorow's PhD supervisor at Harvard was Robert White, one of the closest colleagues of Murray, but Stolorow also attended Murray's classes during the university years that influenced him deeply (personal communication). Atwood was the assistant of eminent affect theorist Silvan Tomkins, who had been a Murray-disciple. Stolorow and Atwood met and became co-authors and friends at Rutgers University as members of Tomkins' personological research group (Atwood & Stolorow, 2013). So their long time cooperation is also a good example of dyadic/intersubjective creativity.

NEO-ANALYTIC AND EXISTENTIAL CONTRIBUTIONS

In this subchapter I would like to refer to some authors who are related to psychoanalysis, although they were not (only) psychoanalysts in the strict sense of the word. But they all represent a dynamic approach to the psychology of personality by accepting the idea of unconscious conflicts, and they all use idiographic, holistic approach in studying psychological phenomena. So I apply the phrase "psychodynamic" to describe their concepts in a broad sense, similar to the late Eugene Taylor (2009). I will take a brief look at Adlerian individual psychology, Jungian analytic psychology, the pre-existential approach of Otto Rank, the neo-analytic perspectives of Erich Fromm and Erik Erikson, and the existential psychology of Rollo May. I will also refer to the question of drug-use and spirituality by citing the ideas of Stanislav Grof.

The first psychoanalyst who left the movement was Alfred Adler, who formed his own school called "individual psychology". The central concept of this theory is the idea of the "Creative Self" for which free will is available; that is why Adler claimed that - opposite to Freud - he never denied the importance and reality of conscious experiences and intentions, artistic visions and intuition (Adler, 2006). In spite of these Adler's theoretical approach to creativity - based on his main term "inferiority complex" - seems to be much more reductionist then Freud's concept. Rollo May once took a group of artists to Adler's private class, and he was surprised, when Adler supposed that none of the group members were artists because they didn't wear glasses. Adler namely presumed that the interest towards painting is the compensation of inferiority feelings because of visual problems (May, 1959).

C. G. Jung's case is more complicated, because Freud wanted him to be his inheritor as the leader of the movement. Their relationship and breaking up is a very complex story; it has been interpreted intensively from different perspectives in the past century (Freud, 1957/1914; Jung, 1962; Alexander, 1990; Kőváry, 2015). Jung's psychology is related to arts in many ways; for example when he constructed his personality typology he – among others - relied on Friedrich Schiller's ideas (Bishop, 2007). In his essay "On the Relation of Analytical Psychology of Arts" Jung (1928) emphasized, that it is no use to investigate the personal context of the artistic creation, because works of art are coming from the collective unconscious. The artist is representing archetypes in artworks using the language of his/her own age, so the psychologist's most important task is to manifest these archetypal contents[13]. So there is no place for personal creativity in Jung's theory, because - according to him - authors of outstanding artistic products like "Faust" or "Zarathustra" are not simple creators but mediators between humans and transpersonal spiritual-intellectual powers. For me this seems to be similar to the functions of the shaman in ancient cultures (Eliade, 1951).

In the psychoanalytic period of his life Otto Rank was one of Freud's closest colleague (exactly his secretary), and as a doctor of literature his most important aim was to integrate psychoanalysis and human sciences (Rank & Sachs, 1912). Because of his concept about the trauma of birth he gradually separated from his master, Freud and his friend, Ferenczi, and had to immigrate to the USA (Liberman, 1985). Creativity played extremely important role in Rank's life and works; one of his most significant later books was "Art and Artist: Creative Urge and Personality Development" (Rank, 1932). He believed that psychoanalysis cannot explain the uniqueness of the personality and the creative urge that belong together genuinely. To create ourselves as individuals and to create something (a work of art) refer to the same psychological phenomenon: man is mortal, but s/he is wishing for immortality, and creative urge is about overcoming this conflict. The first manifestation of this is urge is creating ourselves by selling off infantile dependency. It begins with birth (and separation from the mother as a psychological birth) which is a trauma for everyone, but an artist can exceed this with creative activity. Rank always emphasized the important differences between the creative artist and the neurotic; but if a therapist can help a neurotic person to defeat the anxieties concerning independence, it can lead to the liberation of the creative urge.

Erik H. Erikson - who elaborated the theory of identity and the idea of lifelong personality development - has a special role in psychoanalytic

[13] There is a huge intellectual contradiction in this essay; Jung's starting point is that the only acceptable way a psychologist can approach to arts is the study of the creative process, but, as I referred to it above, he finally concludes that the psychologist has to interpret the works of art in order to manifest the archetypal content.

creativity research. He contributed the development of psychobiography like no one else after Freud by studying how moratorium and identity crisis affected the "outbreak" of creativity in the cases of Martin Luther and Sigmund Freud (Erikson, 1993/1958). In his long and detailed psychobiographies about Luther and Gandhi (Erikson, 1993/1968a) Erikson (1) widened the focus of psychobiography research inserting "spiritual creativity" (Luther, Gandhi) beside artistic and scientific ones, (2) supplemented the life-historical context of the case with cultural-historical contexts, so in his approach "psychobiography" became "psychohistory", and (3) he emphasized the importance of epistemological reflections in psychobiography research by stating that the researcher has to examine his/her personal involvement during the study (Alexander, 2005). In Erikson's epigenetic developmental theory (1993/1968b) "generativity" (including creativity) is one of the most important psychological dimension of mature adult life, which means that creativity is not only about establishing self and identity, but also about the inheritance of personal experiences for further generations.

Erich Fromm's view on creativity (1959) seems to be close to Winnicott's ideas, because he is also talking about creativity as a general attitude. Creative attitude means that we have a chance to see things not according to our prejudices but the way that they really exist. Fromm enumerates five factors as conditions for creative attitude: the capacity to be puzzled, the ability to concentrate, the experience of the "I" (the real self beyond social roles), the ability to accept conflict, and the willingness to be born every day. Concerning this last condition he writes the following: "To be creative means to consider the whole process of life as a process of birth, and not to take any stage of life as a final stage. Most people die before they are fully born. Creativeness means to be born before one dies" (Fromm, 1959, p. 53). I think that this attitude is also there in Hermann Hesse's famous poem "Stages"[14] from his outstanding book "The Glass Bead Game" (1969):

[14] Translated by Richard and Clara Winston (1969).

Be ready, heart, for parting, new endeavor,
Be ready bravely and without remorse
To find new light that old ties cannot give.
In all beginnings dwells a magic force
For guarding us and helping us to live.
(…)
If we accept a home of our own making,
Familiar habit makes for indolence.
We must prepare for parting and leave-taking
Or else remain the slave of permanence.

Fromm's writing was published in a book entitled "Creativity and its Cultivation" (ed. by Harold Anderson, 1959), which is a textbook of *Michigan State's Interdisciplinary Symposia on Creativity,* 1958. The book is containing chapters by outstanding authors like Henry A. Murray, J. P. Guilford, Ernest Hilgard, Margaret Mead, Erich Fromm, Carl Rogers, Abraham Maslow, Rollo May and others. I would briefly refer only to Rollo May here, as he was an eminent representative of North American existential psychology. May was influenced by Freud, Rank and Kierkegaard (May, 1958), and highly interested in arts writing a whole book on creativity ("The Courage to Create", 1994/1972). May (1959) was critical to reductionist psychoanalytic approaches, because it linked creativity to neurosis and sublimation as a defense. May believed that the real foundation of creativity is the encounter with reality; the forms that do not contain this aspect are the versions of pseudo-creativity (escapism, exhibitionism). The encounter is characterized by a high degree of consciousness, while the actualization of creative potential always brings joy and ecstasy. According to May the ecstasy of creation is not irrational (or regressive), it's suprarational: "it involves acting as a total person, with subconscious and unconscious levels in personality acting in some form of unity with conscious levels … It brings intellectual, volitional, and emotional functions into play all together" (p. 64). Creativity is the essence of existence, but not only on individual level; if we want to understand a historical era's psychological dispositions the best that we can do is investigate the arts of that particular age[15].

Talking about "suprarational" levels of consciousness we cannot avoid mentioning the connections between creativity and artificial modifications of consciousness. I referred to the age of Romanticism before, when artists actively started to challenge the boundaries of the conscious self by applying different methods – including drug use. In the first half of the 19th Century Coleridge, De Quincey, Berlioz or Poe used opium, while in the second half – due to the discoveries of Moreau de Tours (Abel, 2005)-hash came into view, followed by cocaine (R L. Stevenson, Freud) (Jay, 2010). It seemed to many that a new age of consciousness was born in the middle of the 20th Century with the spread of psychedelic drugs (mescalin, psylocibin, marihuana, LSD), but longitudinally it turned out that it was not "new", but the last period of the Romantic Order (Doorman, 2006). From the perspective of creativity LSD was the most important psychedelic drug, both artistically (The Beatles, Jimi Hendrix) and scientifically, especially concerning the works of Czeh-American transpersonal psychologist Stanislav Grof. In his book "LSD Therapy" (1980) Grof defined different psychodynamic levels of LSD experiences including the "Freudian", the "Rankian" and the "Jungian". The Freudian is about personal, the Jungian is about the collective unconscious, while the Rankian layer is about re-experiencing "psychological birth" during an LSD trip. The stages of (re)birth aka the "perinatal matrices" - along with "condensed experiences" (COEX-systems) that are related to the stages - have important aesthetic and spiritual[16] aspects. He also cited some LSD-experiments concerning creative artists, drawing the conclusion that psychedelic experiences most of the time influence the inspirational phase of the creative process. As he wrote: "The work of many artists – painters, musicians, writers and poets – who participated in LSD experimentation in

[15] Roy Baumeister (1987) turned this theoretical assumption into practice.

[16] Marion Milner (1987/1956), a representative of British objects relations theories also emphasized that creativity and the experience of the spiritual dimension belong together. Previously I unfolded these relationship in the case of an eminent Hungarian painter, Tivadar Csontváry-Kosztka (Kőváry, 2012).

various countries of the world has been influenced deeply by their psychedelic experiences. Most of them found access to deep sources of inspiration, experienced a striking enhancement and unleashed fantasy, and reached extraordinary vitality, originality and freedom of expression" (Grof, 1980, p. 259). Psychedelic experiences will not make an artist out of anyone, but according to Grof non-artists found that due to psychedelic experience they became more open to previously "incomprehensible" works like the paintings of Picasso or Bosch.

ILLNESS, HEALTH AND CREATIVITY

Thesis: Creativity Is Related to Illness

The question of "creativity and illness vs. health" has its long dialectic story including a thesis (creativity is illness) an antithesis (creativity is health) and a synthesis (creativity is health *and* illness). Ever since Plato and Aristotle drew parallel between mania/melancholia and eminent creativity, there has been an assumption in both in laic and professional discourses about the strong positive correlation and causal relationship between creativity and diseases (Sandblom, 1995). This idea was very popular in the 19th Century in the circle of the artists/philosophers of the Romanticism (Doorman, 2006). The Romantics saw illness as a metaphor (Sonntag, 1978); they believed that illness (especially mental illness) is a special condition, blessing and curse at the same time. The artist gains special, authentic knowledge about human existence via illness by experiencing the deeper dimensions of reality, but suffer, isolation, addiction and early death walk hand in hand with this demonic knowledge. The novels of Thomas Mann – like "Death in Venice", "The Magic Mountain", "Dr. Faustus" - are very good examples of that, so it's not surprising that Mann (1936) welcomed Romanticism influenced Freudian psychoanalysis that also got its deep insights about human psyche by studying illness (neuroses).

The "illness and creativity" narrative also influenced the representatives of the emerging medical discourse in the 19th Century. Psychiatrists and other physicians began to extend the scope of their science to study topics that traditionally had belonged to philosophy, aesthetics or arts (the appearance of the "clinical gaze, Foucault, 1973). Representatives of the medical discourse therefore began to interpret different human phenomena (like eminent creativity, "genius") as they were the manifestations of medical conditions. Italian physician Cesare Lombroso (1891) went so far that he claimed: every genius is mad, and insanity is nothing but the result of organic lesions in the brain. This reductionist and naturalist approach became very popular influencing the emergence of a special research method called pathography. The term was invented by German neurologist Paul Julius Möbius, who wrote "clinical case studies" for example about Rousseau, Schopenhauer and Nietzsche (Schioldann, 2003). Pathography remained popular in the 20th Century, but "madness and genius" researches are still continuing until today although mostly with the use of more positivist research methods (Richards, 1993; Sussman, 2007).

Sigmund Freud believed that pathography cannot say anything new about the artist (Mack, 1971). As I mentioned before, his intention was not to draw parallels between the symptoms of mental problems and the characteristics of works of art; instead he tried to learn how artists gain their knowledge about the unconscious, and how do they transform unconscious fantasies into work of arts (Freud, 1959/1906). In order to understand that he elaborated another method based on psychoanalysis called psychobiography (Kővári, 2011). Although Freud knew that unconscious fantasies are the common sources of dreams, neuroses and creativity, he made a difference by emphasizing that artists have the ability to link their fantasies successfully to the structures of reality (Freud, 1963/1916-17). Some of his followers like Wilhelm Stekel (Bos & Groenendijk, 2007), Maria Bonaparte (Warner, 1991) or Edmund Bergler (1947) were not that prudent, and they identified creativity with neuroticism. With this they unfortunately gave psychoanalytic creativity research a really bad name.

Antithesis: Creativity is Related to Health

Some outstanding psychoanalytic authors in the middle of the 20th Century were more provident, and constructed more "positive" models of creativity claiming that it belongs to the realm of normality. In a previous subchapter I presented the theories of Melanie Klein and Donald Winnicott who are good examples of that. Klein and her followers like Kristeva used the "clinical gaze" more carefully, while Winnicott totally deconstructed the psychopathological context of creativity. Winnicott's endeavors met with the cultural climate of his age, because from the 1950's and 60's we can see the rise of humanistic psychology. Prominent representatives like Rogers and Maslow were both took part in the mentioned Michigan symposia (Anderson, 1959). Rogers (1959) named three important psychological conditions of "constructive creativity": (1) openness to experience, (2) internal locus of evaluation and (3) the ability to toy with elements of concepts, while Maslow (1959) was talking about the creativity of healthy, highly evolved, matured, self-actualizing people.

The tendency that Winnicott, Fromm, Rogers and Maslow started continued in the works of positive psychologists like Mihály Csíkszentmihályi (1996). Positive psychologists are basing their arguments on concepts like "flow", "flourishing" or "happiness". It seems to be a very simplified view on human existence, and it looks like that positive psychologists concerning the philosophical foundations of their work they returned to the utilitarianism of Jeremy Bentham and John Stuart Mill of the 19th Century (Guha & Carson, 2014).

Synthesis: The Bright and Dark Sides of Creativity

To find the golden path between the two above mentioned extremities represented by some psychiatrists, psychoanalysts and positive psychologists, in the end of the 20th and the beginning of the 21st Century researchers began to use more differentiated perspectives in this field. They emphasize that there are different levels of creativity like eminent and everyday creativity or that we have to make a different between the four "C"-s (mini C, little C, pro C and big C) (Kaufman, Beghetto, 2009). Empirical research show that in the cases of everyday creativity or little C psychopathology doesn't play any role, but in the cases of eminent creativity or Big C affective disorders are really common (Richards, 1993). Another new perspective is connected to the evaluation of creativity. In the view of humanistic and positive psychologies creativity appears to be an idolized virtue of Homo sapiens, something like a last bastion of the human spirit in a mechanistic and de-humanized age. But researchers in the beginning of the 21st century (Cropley, Cropley, Kaufman & Runco, 2010) realized that this conceptual one-sidedness is distorting the nature of creativity. If we take all the dimensions of creativity called "the 6 P-s" (*p*erson, *p*rocess, *p*ress, *p*roduct, *p*otential, vs. actualization and *p*ersuasion, see Kozbelt, Beghetto & Runco, 2010) we will see that all of them has its dark side. For example creative products like the atom bomb can destroy mankind (Hecht, 2010), while neuroses and other mental issues belong to the dark side of the creative personality and the creative process. We all have to face existential questions in our life; neurosis is a problematic response to them, while under favorable conditions our efforts will lead us to higher levels of emotional creativity (Averill & Nunley, 2010).

CONCLUSION

In this chapter I intended to unfold how the psychoanalytic approach to creativity evolved in the past 120 years. Psychoanalytic creativity theory has its historical forerunners; the most important direct antecedents were Romanticism and 19th Century medical sciences. Freud's view was unique, because he tried to synthesize these traditions, and this endeavor appeared in his works on creativity. His development in this field can be understood by taking a look at the evolution of his own scientific creativity, which shows the structure of "networks of enterprise". His central idea, "sublimation" seems to be mechanistic theoretically, but he placed the process of sublimating in life historical context, which made this application of psychoanalysis a part of hermeneutic traditions. After his initiations, the development of psychoanalytic creativity research took different ways. American ego-psychologists approached from a formalistic perspective, and clarified the role of different mental activities and personality structures in the creativity process, while the representatives of British object relations theories emphasized the importance of internalized interpersonal aspects. Selfpsychologists and intersubjective theorists demonstrated how works of art and creativity are related to "self-object" functions in order to integrate affective experiences, establishing and keeping up self-coherence. I also tried to point out that some outstanding authors of different psychodynamic trends (individual and analytic psychologies, identity theory, existential or transpersonal psychologies) all contributed to this topic by unfolding different but important aspects of creative personalities and the creative process. Finally I presented that there has been a dialectic movement in the evolution of creativity research. After the "creativity and illness" period (*thesis*, first half of the 20th Century) and the "creativity and health" era (*antithesis*, second half of the 20th Century) by the beginning of the 21st Century, psychologists and psychoanalysts seem to come to a conclusion (*synthesis*) that creativity has different levels and dimensions, and they all have their bright and dark sides.

REFERENCES

Abel, E. L. (2005). Jacques Joseph Moreau (1804–1884). *The American Journal of Psychiatry*, Volume 162, Issue 3, March 2005, pp. 458-458.

Adler, A. (2006). *The General System of Individual Psychology. The Collected Clinical Works of Alfred Adler, Volume 12.* New York, NY: Alfred Adler Institute.

Alexander, I. (1990). The Freud-Jung Relationship: The Other Side of Oedipus and Countertransference. In *Personology. Method and Content in Personality Assessment and Psychobiography* (pp. 115-132). Durham and London, UK: Duke University Press.

Anderson, H. M. (1959). (Ed.). *Creativity and its Cultivation.* New York, NY: Harper & Row.

Arieti, S. (1964). The Rise of Creativity: From Primary to Tertiary Process. *Contemporary Psychoanalysis*, 1964, 1: pp. 51-68.

Aron, L. & A. Harris. (Eds.) (1993). *The Legacy of Sándor Ferenczi.* Hillsdale, NJ: The Analytic Press.

Assoun, P.-L. (2000). *Freud and Nietzsche.* New York, NY: The Athlone Press.

Atwood, G. E. & Stolorow, R. D. (1984). *Structures of Subjectivity.* Hillsdale, NJ: The Analytic Press.

Atwood, G. E. & Stolorow, R. D. (2013). Legacies of the Golden Age. *The Humanistic Psychologist*, 41: pp. 285–300.

Averill, J. R. & E. P. Nunley (2010) Neurosis: The Dark Side of Emotional Creativity. In D. H. Cropley, A. J. Cropley, J. C. Kaufman & M. Runco (Eds.): *The Dark Side of Creativity* (pp. 255-276). Cambridge, NY: Cambridge University Press.

Averill, J. R. & Thomas – Knowles, C. (1991). Emotional Creativity. In K. T. Strongman (Ed.): *International Review of Studies on Emotion, Vol 1.* (pp. 269-299). London, UK.

Bergler, E. (1947). Further Contributions to the Psychoanalysis of Writers. Part I., *Psychoanal. Rev.*, 34:449-468; Part II., 35, pp. 33-50.

Baumeister, R. (1987). How the Self Became a Problem? *Journal of Personality and Social Psychology*, Vol 52. No 1. pp. 163- 176.

Beres, D. (1957): Communication in Psychoanalysis and in the creative process. *Journal of the American Psychoanalytic Association*, 1957. 5: pp. 408-423.

Bishop, P. (2007). *Analytical Psychology and German Classical Aesthetics: Goethe, Schiller and Jung, Volume 1.* London, UK: Routledge.

Bocciagaluppi, M. (1993). Ferenczi's Influence on Fromm. In Aron, L. & A. Harris. (Eds.): *The Legacy of Sándor Ferenczi.* Hillsdale (pp. 185-198). NJ: The Analytic Press.

Bos, J. & Groenendijk, L. (2007). *The Self-Marginalization of Wilhelm Stekel.* The Netherlands: Springer.

Blum, H. (2001). Psychoanalysis and Art, Freud and Leonardo. *Journal of American Psychoanalytic Association*, 49, pp. 1409-1425.

Bollas, Ch. (1978). The Aesthetic Moment and the Search for Transformation. *Annual of Psychoanalysis*, 1978, 6: pp. 385-394.

Chasseguet-Smirgel, J. (1984). Thoughts on the Concept of Reparation and the Hierarchy of Creative Acts. *International Review of Psychoanalysis*, 1984, 11: pp. 399-406.

Cropley, D. H., Cropley, A. J. Kaufman, J. C. & Runco, M. (Eds.) (2010) *The Dark Side of Creativity*. Cambridge, NY: Cambridge University Press.

Dimitrievic, A. (2013). A szelfpszichológia születése a zene szelleméből. (The Birth of Self-psychology from the Spirit of Music.) *Imago Budapest*, 2013/1, pp. 31-42.

Doorman, M. (2006). *A romantikus rend (The Romantic Order)*. Budapest, HU: Typotex.

Durant, W. (1926). *The Story of Philosophy*. New York, NY: Simon & Schuster.

Eagleton, T. (1983). *Literary Theory: An Introduction*. Joboken, NJ: Wiley & Blackwell.

Ehrenzweig, A (1962). A New Psychoanalytic Approach to Aesthetics. *British Journal of Aesthetics* (1962) 2 (4): pp. 301-317.

Eliade, M. (1951). *Shamanism. The Archaic Techniques of Ecstasy*. Princeton, NJ: Princeton University Press.

Elms, A. C. (1994). *Uncovering Lives. The Uneasy Alliance of Biography and Psychology*. New York, NY: Oxford University Press.

Erikson, E. (1993/1958). *Young Man Luther. A Study in Psychoanalysis and History*. New York, NY: W.W. Norton & Company.

Erikson, E. (1993/1968a). *Gandhi's Truth. On the Origins of Militant Nonviolence*. New York, NY: W.W. Norton & Company.

Erikson,, E. (1993/1968b). *Identity, Youth and Crisis*. New York, NY: W.W. Norton & Company.

Erős, F. (2004). *Kultuszok a pszichoanalízis történetében. (Cults in the History of sychoanalysis)*. Budapest, HU: Jószöveg Könyvek.

Ferenczi, S. (1949/1932). Confusion of the Tongues Between the Adults and the Child. *International Journal of Psycho-Analysis*, 30: pp. 225-230.

Ferenczi, S. (2007/1933). A trauma a pszichoanalízisben. (Trauma in Psychoananalysis). In: *Technikai írások (Writings on Technique)*. Budapest, HU: Animula Kiadó.

Fonagy, P. & Target, M. (2003). *Psychoanalytic Theories: Perspective from Developmental Psychopathology.* London, UK: Routledge.

Foucault, M. (1973). *The Birth of the Clinic*. New York, NY: Penguin Books.

Freud, S. (1953/1900). The Interpretation of Dreams. *The Standard Edition of the Complete Psychological Works of Sigmund Freud, Volume IV (1900): The Interpretation of Dreams*. The Hogarth Press and the Institute of Psycho-analysis, London.

Freud, S. (1955/1893-95). Studies on Hysteria. In *The Standard Edition of the Complete Psychological Works of Sigmund Freud, Volume II (1893-1895)*. (pp. 1-323). The Hogarth Press and the Institute of Psycho-Analysis, London.

Freud, S. (1955/1914). The Moses of Michelangelo. *The Standard Edition of the Complete Psychological Works of Sigmund Freud, Volume XIII (1913-1914): Totem and Taboo and Other Work* (pp. 211-236). The Hogarth Press and the Institute of Psycho-analysis, London.

Freud, S. (1955/1919). The Uncanny. *The Standard Edition of the Complete Psychological Works of Sigmund Freud, Volume XVII (1917-1919): An Infantile Neurosis and Other Works* (pp. 217-252). The Hogarth Press and the Institute of Psychoanalysis, London.

Freud, S. (1957/1910). Leonardo da Vinci and a Memory of his Childhood. *The Standard Edition of the Complete Psychological Works of Sigmund Freud, Volume XI. London, UK:* The Hogarth Press and the Institute of Psycho-analysis.

Freud, S. (1957/1914). On the History of the Psycho-Analytic Movement. *The Standard Edition of the Complete Psychological Works of Sigmund Freud, Volume XIV (1914-1916): On the History of the Psycho-Analytic Movement, Papers on Metapsychology and Other*

Works (pp. 6-67). The Hogarth Press and the Institute of Psycho-analysis, London.

Freud, S. (1957/1915). Instincts and their Vicissitudes. *The Standard Edition of the Complete Psychological Works of Sigmund Freud, Volume XIV (1914-1916): On the History of the Psycho-Analytic Movement, Papers on Metapsychology and Other Works* (pp. 109-140). London, UK: The Hogarth Press and the Institute of Psycho-analysis.

Freud, S. (1957/1917). Mourning and Melancholia. *The Standard Edition of the Complete Psychological Works of Sigmund Freud, Volume XIV (1914-1916): On the History of the Psycho-Analytic Movement, Papers on Metapsychology and Other Works* (pp. 237-260). The Hogarth Press and the Institute of Psycho-analysis, London.

Freud, S. (1959/1906). Delusions and Dreams in *Jensen*'s Gradiva. In *The Standard Edition of the Complete Psychological Works of Sigmund Freud, Volume IX (1906-1908): Jensen's 'Gradiva' and Other Work* (p. 3-96). The Hogarth Press and the Institute of Psychoanalysis, London.

Freud, S. (1959/1908). Creative Writers and Day-Dreaming. *The Standard Edition of the Complete Psychological Works of Sigmund Freud, Volume IX (1906-1908): Jensen's 'Gradiva' and Other Works* (pp. 141-154). London, UK: The Hogarth Press and the Institute of Psycho-analysis.

Freud, S. (1959/1926). Inhibitions, Symptoms and Anxiety. *The Standard Edition of the Complete Psychological Works of Sigmund Freud, Volume XIV (1914-1916): On the History of the Psycho-Analytic Movement, Papers on Metapsychology and Other Works* (pp. 77-178). The Hogarth Press and the Institute of Psycho-analysis, London.

Freud, S. (1961/1925). The Resistances to Psycho-Analysis. *The Standard Edition of the Complete Psychological Works of Sigmund Freud, Volume XIX (1923-1925): The Ego and the Id and Other Works* (pp. 211-224). London, UK: The Hogarth Press and the Institute of Psycho-analysis.

Freud, S. (1960/1901), The Psychopathology of Everyday Life. *The Standard Edition of the Complete Psychological Works of Sigmund Freud, Volume VI (1901): The Psychopathology of Everyday Life*. The Hogarth Press and the Institute of Psychoanalysis, London.

Freud, S. (1960/1905). Jokes and their Relation to the Unsconscious. *The Standard Edition of the Complete Psychological Works of Sigmund Freud, Volume VIII (1905): Jokes and their Relation to the Unconscious.* The Hogarth Press and the Institute of Psycho-analysis, London.

Freud, S. (1961/1928). Dostoevsky and Parricide. *The Standard Edition of the Complete Psychological Works of Sigmund Freud, Volume XXI (1927-1931): The Future of an Illusion, Civilization and its Discontents, and Other Works* (pp. 175-198). The Hogarth Press and the Institute of Psycho-analysis, London.

Freud, S. (1961/1930). Civilization and its Discontents. *The Standard Edition of the Complete Psychological Works of Sigmund Freud, Volume XXI (1927-1931): The Future of an Illusion, Civilization and its Discontents, and Other Works* (pp. 59-148). London, UK: The Hogarth Press and the Institute of Psycho-analysis.

Freud, S. (1963/1916-17). *Introductory Lectures on Psycho-analysis (Parts I and II). The Standard Edition of the Complete Psychological Works of Sigmund Freud, Volume XV.* London, UK: The Hogarth Press and the Institute of Psycho-analysis, London.

Freud, S. (1964/1925). An Autobiographical Study. *The Standard Edition of the Complete Psychological Works of Sigmund Freud, Volume XX* (1925-1926) (pp. 1-74). London, UK: The Hogarth Press and the Institute of Psycho-analysis, London.

Fromm, E. (1959). The Creative Attitude. In H. Anderson (Ed.): *Creativity and its Cultivation* (pp. 44-55). New York, NY: Harper & Row.

Gedo, J. (1999). *The Evolution of Psychoanalysis*. New York, NY: Other Press.

Gould, S. J. (1980). *The Panda's Thumb*. New York, NY: Northon & Co.

Gorman, G. J. & Feist, M. E. (Eds.) (2013). *Handbook of Psychology of Science.* New York, NY: Springer Publishing Company.

Gruber, H. E., Bödecker, K. & Wallace, D. (2005). The Case Study Method and Evolving Systems Approach for Understanding Unique Creative People at Work. In H. E. Gruber,& K. Bödecker (Eds): *Creativity, Psychology and the History of Science* (pp. 39-65). The Netherlands: Springer.

Guha, M. & Carson, J. (2014). Positive Psychology, Utilitarianism and the Pursuit of Happiness. *Journal of Mental Health*, 23:4, pp. 159-161

Hagman, G. (2000). The The creative process. *Progress in Self Psychology*, 2000, 16: pp. 277-297.

Hamilton, N. G. (1999). *Self and Others: Object Relations Theory in Practice*. New York, NY: Jason Aronson.

Hartmann, H. (1955). Notes on the Theory of Sublimation. *Psychoanalytic Study of the Child*, 1955, 10: pp. 9-29.

Hecht, (2010). Imagining the Bomb: Robert Oppenheimer, Nuclear Weapons, and the Assimilation of Technological Innovation. In D. H. Cropley, A. J. Cropley, J. C. Kaufman, & M. Runco (Eds.): *The Dark Side of Creativity* (pp. 72-90). Cambridge, NY: Cambridge University Press.

Hermann, I. (1984/1943). *Az ember ősi ösztönei. (Man's Archaic Instincts)*. Budapest, HU: Magvető Kiadó.

Hermann, I. (2007/1930). A tehetség pszichoanalízise (The Psychoanalysis of Talent). *Magyar nyelvű tanulmányok 1911-1933 (Papers in Hungarian)* (pp. 85-97). Budapest, HU: Animula, Kiadó.

Hertz, N. (1979). Freud and the Sandman. In J. V. Harrari (Ed.): *Textual Strategies* (pp. 296-3211). Cornell University Press. New York, NY: Cornell University Press.

Hesse, H. (1969/1943). *The Glass Bead Game: Magister Ludi.* New York, NY: Holt, Rinehart & Winston.

Hilgard, E. (1959). Creativityand Problem Solving. In Harold H. Anderson, H. (Ed.): *Creativity and its Cultivation* (pp. 162-181.) Harper & Row, New York.

Isaacson, K. (2005). Divide and Multiply. Comparative Theory and Methodology in Multiple Case Psychobiography. In W. T. Schultz

(Ed.): *The Handbook of Psychobiography* (pp. 104-112). New York, NY: Oxford University Press.

Jay, M. (2010). *High Society. The Central Role of Mind-Altering Drugs in History, Science and Culture.* Toronto, CA: Park Street Press.

Jones, E. (1953-57). *The Life and Works of Sigmund Freud, Vol. 1-3.* London, UK: The Hogarth Press.

Jung, C. G. (1928). On the Relation of Analytical Psychology of Arts. In *Contributions to Analytical Psychology (pp. 225-250).* London, UK: Kegan Paul, Trench, Tubner & Co.

Jung, C. G. (1962). *Memories, Dreams, Reflections*. New York, NY: Random House.

Karterud, S. (1999). A szelfpszichológia és a hermeneutika. (Self psychology and Hermeneutics). In S. Karterud & J. T. Monsen (1999). *Szelfpszichológia – A Kohut utáni fejlődés. (Self psychology – Development after Kohut)* (pp. 165-177). Budapest, HU: Animula Kiadó.

Karterud, S. & Monsen, J. T. (1999). *Szelfpszichológia – A Kohut utáni fejlődés. (Self psychology – Development after Kohut)*. Budapest, HU: Animula Kiadó.

Kaufman, J. C. & Beghetto, R. A. (2009). Beyond Big and Little: The Four C Model of Creativity. *Review of General Psychology*, Vol. 13, No. 1, pp. 1–12.

Klein, R. H. (1971). Creativity and Psychopathology. A Theoretical Model. *Journal of Humanistic Psychology*, 1971; 11; pp. 40-52.

Koestler, A. (1964). *The Act of Creation*. London, UK: Hutchinson.

Kohut, H. (1980). *Self psychology and the Humanities*. New York, NY: W.W. Norton and Company.

Kohut, H. (2009/1971), *The Analysis of the Self.* Chicago, IL: The University of Chicago Press.

Kohut, H. (2013/1984). *How Does Analysis Cure*? Chicago, IL: The University of Chicago Press.

Kohut, H. (2014/1977). *The Restoration of the Self.* ? Chicago, IL: The University of Chicago Press.

Kozbelt, A., Beghetto, R. A. & Runco, M. A. (2010). Theories of Creativity. In J. C. Kaufman. & R. J. Sternberg (Eds.): *The Cambridge Handbook of Creativity* (pp. 20-47). New York, NY: Cambridge University Press.

Kőváry, Z. (2009). The Enigma of Desire. Salvador Dalí and the Conquest of the Irrational. *PsyArt* 5: 1.

Kőváry, Z. (2011). Psychobiography as a Method. The Revival of Studying Lives: New Perspectives in Personality and Creativity Research. *Europe's Journal of Psychology* Vol. 7. (4), pp. 739-777.

Kőváry, Z. (2012). Látomás és indulat a képzőművészetben. Csontváry és a kreativitás a mai pszichobiográfia tükrében. (Vision and Affect in Fine Arts. Csontváry and Creativity in the View of Modern Psychobiography). *Imágó Budapest*, 2012/1. pp. 35-62.

Kőváry, Z. (2013). Matricide and Creativity: The Case of Two Hungarian Cousin-writers from the Perspective of Contemporary Psychobiography. *International Journey of Creativity and Problem Solving*, 2013, 23 (1), pp. 103-118.

Kőváry, Z. (2015). C.G. Jung's Dream of Siegfried. A Psychobiographical Study. *The Psychoanalytic Reviw,* August, Vol. 102, No. 4: pp. 461-481.

Kőváry, Z. (2016). Psychobiographical Research and Personality Psychological Background of Creativity: The Case of Friedrich Nietzsche. In Moneta, G. B, & Rogaten, J. (eds.): *Psychology of Creativity: Cognitive, Emotional, and Social Processes* (pp. 169-196). New York, NY: Nova Science Publishers.

Kőváry. Z. (2018). Personology (Murray). In V. Zeigler-Hill & T. K. Shackelford (Eds.): *Encyclopedia of Personality and Individual Differences*. Springer International Publishing (in press).

Kris, E. (1955). Neutralization and Sublimation - Observations on Young Children. *Psychoanalytic Study of the Child,* 1955, 10; pp. 30-46.

Kris, E. (2000/1952). *Psychoanalytic Explorations in Art*. Madison, CT: International Universities Press.

Kristeva, J. (1987). On the Melancholic Imaginary. *New Formations*, No. 3, Winter 1987, pp. 5-18.

Kristeva, J. (2001). *Melanie Klein: Matricide as Pain and Creativity*. New York, NY: Columbia University Press.

Kubie, L. (1958). *Neurotic Distortions of the The creative process.* Lawrance, KS: Kansas University Press.

Liebermann, (1985). *Acts of Will. The Life and Works of Otto Rank*. New York, NY: The Free Press.

Loewald, H. (1980). Primary Process, Secondary Process and Language. In *Papers on Psychoanalysis* (pp. 178-206). New Haven, CT: Yale University Press.

Loewald, H. (1988). *Sublimation*. New Haven, CT: Yale University Press.

Lohmann, H. M. (2008). *A huszadik század Ödipusza. Sigmund Freud élete és munkássága. (Oedipus of the 20th Century. The Life and Works of Sigmund Freud).* Budapest, HU: Háttér Kiadó.

Lombroso, C. (1891). *The Man of Genius*. London, UK: Walter Scott.

Mack, J. E. (1971). Psychoanalysis and Historical Biography. *Journal of the American Psychoanalytic Assoiociation*, 1971, 19: pp. 143-179.

Magee, N. (2001). *Wagner and Philosophy*. London, UK: Penguin Books.

Mann Th. (1936), Freud and the Future, in *Essays of Three Decades* (pp. 411-428). New York, NY: Knopf, New York.

Mann, Th. (1965). *Wagner és korunk. (Wagner and Our Age)*. Budapest, HU: Zeneműkiadó.

Martindale, C. (1978). The Evolution of English Poetry. *Poetics,* 7(2):pp. 231-248.

May, R. (1958). The Origins and Significance of Existential Movement in Psychology. In May, R., Angel, Ernest & Ellenberger, H. (Eds): *Existence. A New Dimenison in Psychiatry and Psychology* (pp. 8-36.). New York.

May, R. (1959). The Nature of Creativity. In Anderson, H. (Ed.): *Creativity and its Cultivation* (pp. 55-69). New Yor, NY: Harper & Row.

May, R. (1994/1972). *Courage to Create*. New Yor, NY: W. W. Norton & Company.

McAdams, D.P. (1988). Biography, Narratives and Lives: an Introduction. In D. P. McAdams & R. Ochberg, R. (Eds.): *Psychobiography and Life Narratives* (pp. 1-18). Durham, NC: Duke University Press.

Milner, M. (1987/1956) Psychoanalysis and Art. In *The Supressed Madness of Sane Men* (pp. 156-180). Hove and New York, NY: Brunner-Routledge.

Modell, A. (1970). The Transitional Object and the Creative Act. *Psychoanalytic Quarterly*, 1970, 39: pp. 240-250.

Mitchell, S. & Black, M. (1995). *Freud and Beyond. A History of Modern Psychoanalytic Thought*. New York, NY: Basic Books.

Nietzsche, F. (1968/1889). *The Will to Power*. New York, NY: Vintage Books.

Nietzsche, F. (1986/1878-1880). *Human, All Too Human*. Cambridge, UK: Cambridge University Press.

Nietzsche, F. (2005/1888). The Case of Wagner. A Musician's Problem. In *The Anti-Christ, Ecce Homo, Twilight of the Idols and Other Writings* (pp. 231-252). Cambridge, UK: Cambridge University Press.

Noy, P. (1972). About Art and Artistic Talent. *International Journal of Psycho-Analysis*, 53: pp. 243-249.

Paneth, G. (1985). Gnosztikus és pszichoanalitikus elemek Richard Wagner zenedrámáiban. (Gnostic and Psychoanalytic Elements in the Musical Dramas of Richard Wagner. In *A labirintus járataiban. Pszichiátria, kultúra, klinikum* (In the Labyrinth. Psychiatry, Culture, Clinics). (pp. 150-176). Budapest, HU: Magvető Könyvkiadó.

Plato (2002). *Phaidros*. New York, NY: Oxford University Press.

Rank, O. & Sachs, H. (1916). *The Significance of Psychoanalyisis for the Mental Sciences*. New York, NY: The Nervous and Mental Disease Publishing Company.

Rank, O. (1932). *Art and Artist*. New York, NY: W. W. Norton & Company.

Rogers, C. (1959). Toward a Theory of Creativity. In Harold M. Anderson (Ed.): *Creativity and its Cultivation* (pp. 69-82). New York, NY: Harper & Row.

Rolland, R. (1931). *Goethe and Beethoven*. London, UK: Hamilton Ltd.

Richards, R. (1993). Creativity, Eminent Creativity and Psychopathology. *Psychological Inquirly*, 1993, No. 3, pp. 212-217.

Rosenblum, R. (2012).“In More Favourable Circumstances”: Ambassadorsof the Wound. In Judit Székács-Weisz & Tom Keve (Eds.): *Ferenczi for Our Time* (pp. 117-148). London, UK: Karnac.

Rudnytsky, P. (1987): *Freud and Oedipus.* New York, NY: Columbia University Press.

Safranski, R. (2014). *Romanticism: A German Affair*. Evanston, IL: Northwestern University Press.

Sandblom, Ph. (1995). *Creativity and Disease*. London, UK & New York NY: Marion Boyars.

Sandler, J. & Joffe, W.G. (1966). On Skill and Sublimation. *Journal of American Psychoanalytic Association,* 1966, 14: pp. 335-355.

Scheler, M. (1968/1928). *The Human Place in the Cosmos*. Evanston, IL: Northwestern University Press.

Schioldann, J. A. (2003). What is Pathography? *The Medical Journal of Australia*, 2003 178 (6): p. 303.

Schivelbusch, W. (1994). *Az írástudók alkonya. (The Twilight of the Intellectuals)*. Budapest, HU: Akadémiai Kiadó.

Schopenhauer, A. (1966/1818-19). *The World as Will and Representation Vol 1&2*. Mineola, NY: Dover Publications.

Segal, H. (1988/1964). Introduction to the Work of Melanie Klein. London, UK: The Hogarth Press.

Stern, D. (2008/1985). *The Interpersonal World of the Infant*. New York NY: Basic Books.

Stolorow, R. D. (2011). *World, Affectivity, Trauma. Heidegger and Post-Cartesian Psychoanalysis.* New York, NY & London, UK: Routledge – Taylor & Farncis Group.

Stolorow, R. D: & Atwood, G. E. (1992). *Contexts of Being*. Hillsdale, NY: The Analytic Press.

Stolorow, R. D., Atwood, G. E. & Brandchaft. B. (1994). *The Intersubjective Perspective*. New York, NY: Jason Aronson.

Stolorow, R. D., Brandchaft, B. & Atwood, G. E. (1987). *Psychoanalytic Treatment: An Intersubjective Approach.* Hillsdale, NJ: The Analytic Press.

Sulloway, F. (1979). *Freud, Biologist of the Mind.* New York, NY: Basic Books.

Sussman, A. (2007). Mental Illness and Creativity. A Neurological View of the "Tortured Artist". *Sanford Journal of Neuroscience*, Volume 1, Issue 1, pp. 21-24.

Székács-Weisz, J. & Keve, T. (Eds.) (2012). *Ferenczi for Our Time.* London, UK: Karnac.

Taylor, E. (2009). *The Mystery of the Personality. A History of Psychodynamic Theories.* London, UK c New York, NY: Springer.

Tonnesmann, M. (2012). Early Emotional Development: Ferenczi to Winnicott. In Judit Székács-Weisz & Tom Keve (Eds.): *Ferenczi for Our Time* (pp. 29-42). London, UK: Karnac.

Trilling, L. (1963). Art and Neurosis. In William Phillips (ed.): *Art and Psychoanalysis* (pp. 502-520). Cleveland and New York, NY: Meridian Books.

Walsh, R. T. G., Th. Teo, A. Baydala (2014). *A Critical History and Philosophy of Psychology.* Cambridge, UK: Cambridge University Press.

Warner, S. L. (1991). Princess Marie Bonaparte, Edgar Allan Poe, and Psychobiography. *Journal of American Academic Psychoanaysis.*, 19: pp. 446-461.

Wertheimer, M. (1938). The Syllogism and Productive Thinking. In W. D. Ellis (Ed.): *A Source Book of Gestaltpsychology* (pp. 274-282). London, UK: Kegan Paul, Trench Tubner & Co.

Winnicott, D.W. (1965) A Personal View of the Kleinian Contribution. *The Maturational Processes and the Facilitating Environment* (pp.171-178). London, UK: Karnac Books.

Winnicott, D. W. (2005/1971). *Playing and Reality.* London, UK: Routledge.

Wittkower, R. & Wittkower, M. (1963). *Born Under Saturn. The Character and Conduct of Artists.* New York, NY: Random House.

In: Psychoanalytic Theory
Editors: K. Martin and M. Siegward
ISBN: 978-1-53612-484-2

Chapter 3

EARLY TRAUMATIC EXPERIENCES AND SYMBOLIZATION: WORKING WITH PRIMITIVE MENTAL FUNCTIONINGS

Paola Solano, MD[1,*] and Luca Quagelli, PhD[2,†]

[1]Department of Neurosciences, Rehabilitation, Ophthalmology, Genetics, Maternal and Child Health, Section of Psychiatry and Psychodynamic Psychotherapy, University of Genoa, Italy

[2]Doctoral School Research in Psychoanalysis, Paris VII-Diderot University, Paris, France

ABSTRACT

Freud and Klein maintained that there is no trauma outside the individual's omnipotence. However, Winnicott described the existence of primitive mental functionings stemming from early traumatic impingements that shatter the baby's area of omnipotence that persist

---

* Correspondence: Paola Solano, MD, Email: paola.solano@alice.it.
† Luca Quagelli, PhD, Email: Lucaquagelli@hotmail.com.

throughout adulthood. These areas of primitive mental functioning co-exist, often in a split off and fragmented way, with more mature areas of the personality causing severe impairments in the sense of self and in the capacity of thinking and symbolization. When there is failure in the original encounter with the object the traces of that early trauma cannot be repressed and remain in the mind as registrations of perceptions which, in Freud's words, are formed by raw proto-emotions (such as body-centred sensations, tones, rhythms and postures). Therefore, these traces can emerge during treatment only through non-verbal communicative modes because they have never reached word presentation. Recent contributions on these phenomena suggest that registration of perceptions lie in the mind in negative as 'voids' or 'psychic holes' that - to quote Green - significantly destabilize the mental apparatus. Nowadays, work with borderline and psychotic patients has become more common in psychoanalytic practice and clinicians have to face and deal with unrepresented mental areas seeking transformation and figuration. In this chapter, firstly we present some recent theoretical understandings on the origin of unrepresented mental areas and their relationship with early traumatic experiences. Secondly, we introduce and discuss some technical issues that foster the development of the first representation of early traumatic experiences within the analytic couple, i.e., the role of the setting; the affective response to the patient's communications in the analyst's bodily countertransference and reverie as well as the role and features of interpretation while working with these patients.

Keywords: unrepresented mental states, symbolization, early trauma, primitive mental functioning, psychoanalytic technique, free associative activities, interpretative experiences, bodily countertransference

INTRODUCTION

For a long time psychoanalysis stood as a theory of symbolization grounded on the meta-psychology of absence. Sexual theories of children together with the construction/re-construction of the family romance (Freud, 1909) stood at the centre of psychoanalytic work. However, this took the structuring of boundaries between "me/not me" for granted. Freud assumed the difference between "me/not me", as well as the entanglement of the drives, as a “starting point”, thus difficulties could arise from its acknowledgement and acceptance, but not from its establishment.

However, in contemporary clinical practice, it is quite common to meet patients with borderline or psychotic functioning that are present to different extends being sometimes present just in pockets. In these mental functionings, the very structure of thought and the thinking process is altered and there is no differentiation between the conscious and the unconscious, between sleeping and waking, between self and other (Bion, 1962). Symbolization is impaired to different degrees according to the state of the ego’s relationships with its objects, ranging from isolated areas of unrepresented mental states - voids and “psychic holes” (Green, 1983, p.146) - to whole psychotic structures. Interestingly, studies focusing on the nature of unrepresented psychic nuclei show an intimate relationship with early traumatic experiences that occurred during the first encounter with the object which impaired or prevented the containment process from taking place - thus hindering the possibility of accessing transitionality to different extents. Therefore, unrepresented nuclei are constituted by “never symbolized feelings and emotions” that, because of their intensity and violence, could not undergo the process of symbolization and, therefore, could not be repressed. Rather, they remain inscribed in negative in the baby’s mind as psychic nuclei that are “too full of excitement” and “voids of representation”. These are unphantomable and unbearable experiences (Bergstein 2016) that cannot be verbally expressed nor dreamt because of the object’s failure to contain and transform them.

However, these nuclei harbour communicative potential that can come forward during treatment through non-verbal communicative modes such as unconscious-to-unconscious communication, bodily feelings and somatizations. Consequently, the classical psychoanalytic technique has to carefully consider these peculiarities and develop effective strategies to allow therapists to make contact with, understand and transform these extreme forms of psychic pain that are communicated through more primitive registers than the usual verbal one.

This, we believe, is one of the most cogent and urgent challenges for contemporary and future psychoanalysis. In this chapter, first we present some recent theoretical understandings on the origin of unrepresented mental areas and their relationship with early traumatic experiences. Second, we present and discuss some technical issues that foster the development of a first representation of early traumatic experiences in the analytic couple, i.e., the role of the setting; the working through of the patient's communications through the analyst's bodily countertransference and reverie. Eventually, the role and features of free association and interpretation in the work with these patients will be explored and discussed.

On the Origin of Unrepresented Mental States: Some Theoretical Understandings

Psychoanalytic contributions focusing on primitive mental functionings underline the importance of the early mother-infant relationship and the object's capacity to offer "good enough" containment for the infant's proto-emotions in order to promote symbolization and the development of the boundary between me and not me. In his early writings, Freud (1986) suggested the idea of the existence of raw proto-emotions inscribed in the mind simply as "perceptive traces" that could not reach representation - thus heralding the modern conceptualization of unrepresented mental states to some extent. However, this idea was never developed any further and he considered it only phenomenologically. For instance, in a letter to Fliess written on the 6th December 1896, Freud (ibid.) describes a model for memory, according to which every event has "at least a triple registration" (ibid., p.234). In addition to the better known thing-presentation *(Sachvorstellung)* and word- presentation *(Wortvorstellung)*, Freud put forward the existence of a third early registration called "indication of perception" (ibid., p.234) arranged according to association by simultaneity and contiguity. Though still present in *The Interpretation of Dreams*, registrations of "indication of perception" are apparently overlooked in Freud's subsequent work, being simply differentiated from other unconscious representative traces because of the degree of cathexis. Recently, the importance of early perceptual traces has been rediscovered and different types of them were described, e.g., formal signifiers (Anzieu, 1990), demarcation signifiers (Rosolato, 1985) and pictograms (Aulagnier, 1975).

Winnicott (1971) was the first to explore the nature of these indications of perceptions formed by raw proto-emotions and suggested a link between them and the failure of the early mother- infant relationship and encounter. Hindrances and failures can take place at any time during the complex encounter with the object when the boundary "me/not me" has to be built as a result of interplay between the two partners – mother and infant – who have to establish, construct and organize it dialectically. This process is at the same time both intra- and inter-subjective and is made up of a ballet of presence and absence. To be able to cathect his bodily sensations, the infant needs both an object and the object's work. This object is a paradoxical object in the sense that it is both narcissistic (i.e., object of narcissism in Green's sense) and "double of the self" (Roussillon, 2011, p.136), which in keeping its alterity though mirroring the self, helps in regulating it - Roussillon's "primary double homosexuality" (ibid., p.135). Hence, the object is at the same time something to be symbolized (register of the "use of the object") and a tool for symbolization (register of "relationship with the object"). In particular, it introduces "otherness" which has to be symbolized with the help of work that has to be done with the object.

The primal psychic matter, that is a registration of experience which has not undergone any further transformation except for that required for the inscription in the psychism itself, largely derives from bodily sensations of the primal encounter with the object. "To grasp itself *(se saisir d'elle-meme)"* (Roussillon, 1999, p.224), the primal psychic matter has to be presented to the subject from the outside by an object able to receive and re-present the primal hallucination. Thus, this process has to be "mediated" and the object has to "mirror" the primal psychic matter and look for signification that largely derives from the encounter with itself. The perceptual similarity between the nature of the trace and object fosters the transference of primal psychic matter in it, akin to Winnicott's found/created process. In this process, the object has to let itself be used and creatively tolerate the paradox underlying the transference of this early experience to allow the infant to develop the capacity of self-reflection, which is grounded in the mother's early psycho-somatic mirroring. "In the choreographies" played by and within the mother-infant couple "a whole series of sensations are attuned, communicated, conveyed, shared and, at the same time, regulated. The self's cathexis of the body and bodily sensations depends on the encounter with the cathexis of the reflection that the object sends back through its attunement" (Roussillon, 2011, pp.136-137). This attunement has to be not only reciprocal and unconscious but above all non-modal, i.e., "not exactly the same", but "alike" (Stern, 1985). The capacity of the mother's body to harmoniously attune with her baby's movements and sensory states and vice versa allows the latter to bodily experience a reflection of its own "potential beauty" (Roussillon, 2011, p.139).

Different kinds of impingements can take place during this process and alter or undermine the development of the capacity of symbolization which, however, is usually impaired focally rather than globally. Therefore, the experiences belonging to this spectrum are usually isolated in split off nuclei and coexist in the mind juxtaposed to other modes of functioning which have better representational capacities. In this way, we can imagine different levels and forms of unrepresented states ranging from proper unrepresented mental states to weakly represented states that are inscribed in the mind as bodily experiences (Busch 2017; Busch and Sandberg 2014). Frequently, different degrees of impairment in the capacity of symbolization derive from failures of the object being an "environmental mother" who, because of her own narcissistic sufferings, cannot carefully accompany, respect and transform her baby's early rhythm. In these situations, a dysrhythmia is likely to develop, in which the inevitable discrepancies between the partners are experienced as painful intrusions and cannot be regulated by the mother's attunement (Roussillon, 1991). Therefore, the cathexis of the baby's own perceptions and sensations is hindered to different extents due to the object's difficulty in accepting and tolerating them without forcing her own experiences back into the baby, who, in order to survive, retreats from this primary traumatic experience by splitting his own subjective psychic life. In this way, the baby does not feel the trauma anymore and is "decentralized" (Roussillon, 2011, p. 12) from his own subjective experiences. Psychically, he is not there anymore but the traumatic traces lie in the unconscious.

From a different though complementary vertex, Bion (1962) developed a theory of thinking which had profound effects both on the conceptual and technical repertoire of psychoanalysis. Thoughts and thinking, the latter being developed "by the pressure" (ibid., p.179) of the former, were to be considered separately. Psychopathology could derive from the altered development of each or both. The development of thoughts and thinking involves both the infant's capacity for tolerating frustrations and his early relationship with his object. The capacity for tolerating frustrations, such as the experience of an absent breast (realization of "no breast") allows the development of a thought, thus avoiding paranoid anxieties. Furthermore, thinking has a deep relational quality since it derives from the early experience of the relationship with an object capable of receiving, tolerating, transforming and eventually giving back projected anxieties in a more tolerable form. According to this model, through the repeated experience of being contained, the infant can introject not only what was contained, but also the containing object itself together with his alpha function. This enables the mind to contain its own anxieties, to think, to symbolize and to develop a differentiation between the conscious and unconscious. For a normal development to take place, Bion underlined the importance of the mother's capacity for reverie, that is "a state of mind which is open to the reception of any 'object' from the loved object and is therefore capable of the reception of the infant's projective identifications whether they are felt to be good or bad" (Bion, 1962a, p. 36). Thus, Bion conceptualizes thinking not as an abstract mental process, but as a human link and emotional experience, of trying to know oneself or someone else (O'Shaughnessy, 1981).

Both Winnicott's and Bion's models about the origin of unrepresented mental areas and development of thought underline the role of the primal relationship and the deep relational quality of the process that leads to the development of symbolization. Therefore, therapists and analysts should consider carefully the peculiarities of these primitive mental functionings and be able to listen to communicative modes that deeply differ from the usual verbal ones in order to be able to recognize, receive, tolerate, transform and give the first representation of these intense mental states. Hence, technical issues concerning the work with unrepresented mental states should be taken into account because of their peculiarities that foster the first process of symbolization.

Working with Unsymbolized Mental States

Work with severely disturbed patients who have wide unrepresented mental areas is often hard and challenging. A large body of literature has investigated technical issues to make contact with and promote transformation while working with these patients since the classical psychoanalytic device implies quite a developed capacity for symbolization and does not suit these mental functionings. For instance, describing the psychoanalytic device, Freud (1913) suggested that patients should be imagined as "travellers sitting next to the window of a railway carriage and describing to someone inside the carriage the changing views which [they] see outside" (ibid., p. 135). This apparently simple statement implies that the patient can develop a triple intrapsychic transference. First, the train has to proceed, that is, drives have to produce a psychic movement promoting a first libidinal transference in the motor and emotional field. Second, the motor field has to be transformed into images (thing presentation). To facilitate this transformation the classical analytic device forbids any movement together with the analyst's view so that the interplay between inner images can reproduce the phantasmatic world and its dynamics. Eventually, visual thing presentations, so obtained, have to be translated into word presentations so that they can be addressed to the analyst. In the classical psychoanalytic device, both fundamental rule and setting sustain a process of transformation of the psychic apparatus into an apparatus for linguistic symbolization (secondary symbolization), where the former puts into words what the device communicates through actions. Thus, the device contains a materialized "theory" of symbolization that is "acted" in its practice through its rules and modalities (Quagelli and Solano, 2016), which make the patient learn what symbolization is accepted and what kind of material is considered "significant" in treatment (Roussillon, 2012). The analytic setting suggests that symbolization can be achieved only through words, and the analyst's position, out of the patient's view, asks patients to deal with absence, that implies first and foremost the symbolization of absence when the object is really absent or, at least, when the patient is alone in the presence of the object. However, this device does not suit mental states characterized by the presence of unmentalized nuclei deriving from early traumatic experiences that cannot be integrated in the psyche because the mental apparatus cannot transform them but can only split them off in order to handle their destructiveness. Thus, the psyche cannot transform these motor, perceptive and proto-emotional elements into visual images to achieve thing presentation, and, at the same time, certain thing presentations cannot be "translated" into language. Therefore, it is central to remember that these patients come to sessions to make the analyst feel what they cannot feel and represent; they unconsciously "show" and "act" what they cannot say. Consequently, analysts should attempt to work through their intense countertransferential feelings stimulated by intense projective identification in order to receive and transform these proto-emotions that are looking for a mind to represent them. For instance, working with these primitive areas makes the analyst not just feel and think "with" the patient, but to feel and think "for" the patient. Here, we analyze some central features concerning techniques used while working with unrepresented mental areas.

On Non-Verbal Communicative Modes and the Role of Language

First, we present some metapsychological considerations about "communicative" modes through which the unsymbolised emerges in sessions together with some possible adaptations of the analyst's free floating attention.

In these clinical situations where no word presentation has taken place, the communicative properties of verbalized material and of free association have to be carefully considered, since words may serve different purposes including providing "more an opaque screen than a link enabling communication" (Bion, 1979, p.467). Thus, the very function of language can be perverted and language – paradoxically – becomes a defensive tool against true expression and symbolization! Therefore, verbalizing and associating do not always mean thinking (Bronstein, 2002). Hence, we can recognize "words" and "beyond words communication" (O'Shaughnessy, 1982, p. 139), which can often be detected in the transference. "Beyond words communication", using more primitive modes of communication enable more primitive aspects of the patient to be expressed in treatment, whereas words can reflect a primitive defensive organization (ibid.). Similarly, though using a different model of the mind, McDougall (1975) describes situations in which language is used "as an act" (ibid., p.178) and has little in common with the language of free association. In such cases, the manifest communication does not allow the uncovering of any unconscious scenario (e.g., pertaining to infant sexuality), but appears empty and "meaningless at all levels" (ibid., p.177) to the analytic ear. At the same time, however, the analyst often feels disturbed or unbalanced and his capacity to think is put at stake by "something" (ibid., p.178) that resembles more a baby's desperate cry than actual communication. This mode of functioning is expressively described by Alvarez (1992) in her work concerning an autistic child who used to repeat his stories over and over again during treatment. She wrote: "my mistake in the early years [of his treatment] had been to think that because he was repeating [the same stories over and over again], they still had as yet an ununderstood meaning.

In fact, what meaning there was, lay in the sensual qualities of the words themselves, not in the stories. [Later], I simply began to know that the stories were utterly dead" (ibid., p.52). Thus, it is through the sensuous-perceptive-motoric matrix of the encounter with the object – i.e., with the analyst during treatment – that the first psychic unrepresented inscriptions can emerge in the session.

Consistently with these understandings, Roussillon (2011) underlined the significance of the drives as messengers, whose message can be conveyed (re-presented) through different modes in the treatment such as bodily states, gestures, facial expressions, postures, prosody and affects according to the mode in which it had been inscribed the patient's psyche-soma. These understandings question the historical dichotomy between thought and action that is also supported by the classical psychoanalytic device where actions occur only through language. However, this perspective which understands "actions" as mere emotional discharges is controversial, because a large number of authors hypothesized actions to have specific communicative potentialities. These understandings bridge thought and action by recognizing a possible linking function and communicative property even in the latter, "actions entail a memory and a degenerated proto-narration of pre-verbal experiences and archaic modes of relating" (Roussillon 2009, p.23). Similarly, Bion recognizes the existence of "embryological sensuous memories" (Bion 1977) that lie, as inaccessible states of the mind, beyond *cs* and *ucs* experiences and are recognizable by a careful and intuitive ear, able to listen to other registers besides the verbal and visual ones that fall out of the normal "spectrum of the visible" (Bion 1967). For instance, Bion makes use of the spectrum of electromagnetic wavelengths, visible to all of us, that fall between ultraviolet and infrared, to refer to a realm of mental life that is verbally communicable and recognizes the existence of "emotional wavelengths" that fall out of the normal perceptible spectrum. Bion underlines the communicative property of these out–of –the –visible-spectrum wavelengths and encourages analysts to be receptive and sensitive to them while wondering whether it would be possible for analysts to make "some corresponding extensions of their technical ability, or mental capacity, to take in a little bit more of the invisible aspects of the spectrum" (Bion 1967, p.60). The communicative property of these experiences falling beyond the visible spectrum should be looked for in very primitive registers, which are not verbal nor visual yet, but could lie in "an awareness of muscular movements [...], in smell, tactile impressions" (ibid., p.61). Importantly, through this primitive register very archaic experiences, such as embryological intuitions, could be retrieved and bridged with consciousness. Therefore, analysts have to listen beyond what is being said, beyond the noises of the uttered words to be able to "intuit" (Bion 1970) what the patient's mind cannot yet realize.

The Role of Countertransference in the Path towards Representation

Reverie, "a principal form of re-presentation of the unconscious – largely intersubjective – experience" (Ogden, 1997, p.727), has been suggested as a fundamental tool in order to begin the transformation process of raw proto-emotions since it allows non-represented experiences to be made into verbally symbolic metaphors. The analyst's capacity for reverie, akin to the early mother's reverie, is a way to achieve a first representation of unconscious nameless anxieties. Among the different products of reverie, sudden visual images that spring to the analyst's mind during the session without being "worked out" are particularly valuable not only to understand the current analytical situation, but also as a "third" in the sense of Winnicott's transitional space (Birksted- Breen, 2012). These visual images (ideograms) allow a first "digestion" of raw emotional experiences, giving them a first representation, which have to be further elaborated by the alpha function to become dream work (Bion, 1992). Ideograms resulting from reverie are a "meeting ground" between the analyst's symbolic thinking and the analysand's concrete thought, although they already entail a first development towards symbolization. According to Freud's model that would be the first step towards representation, i.e., from the indication of perception to thing-presentation. How are these early representations built up in the analyst's mind? How does the unfreezing of psychic life take place in clinical practice through the elaboration of psychic voids, session by session?

Working with these primitive mental states the analyst is confronted with an intense countertransferential reaction, akin to those provoked by the desperate cry of a baby that could, make him experience dreadful anxieties and unbalancing emotional storms deep inside himself which threaten his capacity to retain his analytic function and attitude. Furthermore, these patients have apparently renounced the communicative function of words and are rarely reached by interpretations formulated in terms of projection/introjection. This means the analyst is likely to feel helpless, stuck in a concrete mental functioning and incompetent to the point of questioning his human and professional skills. These are complex situations that were historically believed to be unanalysable. However, recent contributions suggest that the possible key to understanding and therapeutic action is in what is enacted rather than in what is spoken.

For instance, Roussillon (1999) suggests the existence of a "*transfert par retournement*" [transference by reversion] (ibid., p.14) in which the patient, through projective identification, makes the analyst experience - in a reversal from passive to active - what he suffered without being able to think. In these situations, Roussillon argues that an early interpretation of aggressiveness would not be of help since the boundaries between inside/outside and subject/object have not yet been developed.

In order to work effectively with these primitive areas, analysts have to feel and think "for" the patient and this implies that they interact with their own areas of private madness and, resonating with the patient's primitive areas, can take charge of the mental pain that the patient could not experience when the break down occurred.

Winnicott (1949) noticed that traces of early traumatic events could appear during treatment, though in a disguised way. They often appear as flowery memories, in which abundant details were added in subsequent developmental stages. The analyst therefore, should pay attention to the main underlying affect, which refers to the early trauma. It should be reminded that après-coup modifications occur to a lesser extent in split and denied perceptual traces than in repressed material, so "the main underlying affect does not lie" (ibid., p.74). Therefore, following the affects in the countertransference the analyst should suggest hypothesis aiming at a reconstruction of the historical reality of the primitive failure in meeting the object. This should not be understood just in terms of projections, but rather as "what historically has persecuted and enslaved the patient" (Roussillon, 1991, p. 248). Approaching the patient's historical reality, as presented in dreams, association and – above all – actions, allows the analyst to formulate constructions closer to the patient's true identity and true Self. The creation of a safe space where "true" constructions can take place is usually the result of many years of hard work. Before a "true" reconstruction of the historical reality can occur, thought should be constructed in areas where it never existed otherwise the patient would not be able to "see" his own historical reality, thus to exist.

The Role of the Setting in the Symbolization Process

Drawing on Freud's understandings and conceptualization of the setting, Winnicott (1954) realized that there was a substantial difference in the way the setting was perceived by neurotic and non-neurotic patients. For instance, in the treatment of neurotic patients who could internalize the experience of "the early mothering situation" (ibid., p. 284), the symbolic meaning of the setting could be taken for granted during treatment. Differently, when working with non-neurotic patients, who experienced failure in their primal emotional development, the setting had a different role. In particular, the setting embodies the reliability, predictability, and safety that the infant could not experience in its primal encounter with the object and, consequently, the couch does not *represent* the analyst's body anymore, but *is* the analyst himself because the as-if dimension has not been achieved yet. Consequently, one should think of non-neurotic mental functionings as being ruled by primitive needs (ego's needs) rather than desires and the setting has to provide a space "safe to be" (Little, 1985, p.

16), where patients can feel that they can start to exist. Thus, the analytic setting becomes the repository of symbiosis and it is where the patient's unrepresented traumatic areas are projected and, therefore, indifferentiation and lack of boundaries between self/other prevail. In this way, the framing function of the analytic setting acquires more relevance according to the state of the internal frame that circumscribes the representative mental space (Quagelli and Solano, 2016). However, the fundamental holding function of the setting is likely to remain silent and unnoticed until, for different reasons, it is modified or broken even by small modifications that can cause violent and disorganizing reactions (Bleger, 1967). A large body of literature reports how minimal changes in the setting, such as changing the position of the objects in the consulting room, could reactivate experiences of failure in the primal encounter when the object could not be found and the infant had attempted to create it. Thus, the setting comes into the foreground and patient and analyst feel that something hostile, something against the setting, is taking place (Green, 1975). Importantly, the working through process of these traumatic proto-emotions allows their gradual representation and introjection into the patient's psyche that leads to a more mature mental functioning.

Concerning the arrangement of the setting, it has been suggested that the vis-à-vis would be better than the lying position since it prevents the patients from a too disorganized regression. Moreover, sensing and perceiving the analyst's face and body is of particular importance for these patients, whose failure lies in their early meeting with the object. This facilitates the mirroring of proto-emotions, gestures and "thoughts without thinker" that the patient could not successfully put into words on his own (Roussillon, 2005).

Free Association in the Work with Unrepresented Mental States: on Enacted Free Association

The method of free association was conceptualized by Freud along with the first topic (i.e., the unconscious, conscious, preconscious) when unconscious material was thought to correspond to repressed material. Therefore, significant limitations are shown when applied to the treatment of patients with unrepresented mental areas who do not have a clear established differentiation between the conscious and the unconscious and whose early traumatic experiences could not be repressed because they never reached the stage of word presentation. Thus, broader conceptualizations of free association are needed which are better suited to working with these kind of patients. Drawing on Klein's understanding of a function similar to free association in "enacted" activity, such as play in children (Klein, 1926), the concept of "free associative activities" has been put forward (Solano and Quagelli, 2015). For example, the model of free associative activities extends the current conceptualization of free association to encompass expressive modes other than verbalized material, such as sudden actions (*Einfalle*), affect foreclosure, reverie products that spring to the analyst's mind (e.g., pictograms), massive projective identification and even enactments recognizing their communicative function. During work with primitive mental functioning, where the symbolizing function is not yet developed, these phenomena could be the only way through which the mind can communicate. Moreover, all these mental events are "free" in the sense that they are ruled by an unconscious determinism and not subjected to any conscious criticism and lead to the unfolding of the patient's inner world. Therefore, they could be considered under a broadened umbrella of free association.

Interpretation during Work with Unrepresented Mental States: on Interpretative Experiences

Interpretation is one of the central tools used by psychoanalysts to promote transformation. Classically, it has been used as a "synonym for making what is unconscious conscious" (Strachey, 1934, p. 281) although the role and function of interpretation vary according to how the mind and psychic apparatus are conceptualized. Therefore, when working with patients with no clear differentiation between conscious and unconscious or self/other, the role and features of interpretation should be carefully considered because they lack the basis of classical conceptualizations. In these clinical situations verbal interpretations, albeit correct as far as the content is concerned, would entail a certain amount of aggression and violence because of the imposition of impoverishing and oversimplified abstractions arising from translating the current emotional experience into words. Moreover, emotionally cathected words belong only to the analyst's register and would deepen the gap between the patient and analyst. Premature verbalization of raw proto-emotions could clash with the patient's mental functioning which is unable to receive words with their symbolizing function and potentiality. Thus, interpretation could risk becoming a concrete object obstructing rather than facilitating evolution and could repeat in the sessions the trauma caused by early environmental impingements. Hence, the classical conceptualization of "interpretation" should be broadened as to include "interpretative experiences" (Quagelli and Solano, 2016) that are formed by the analyst's capacity for reverie and containment coupled with the stability and reliability of the setting that plays an active role in allowing the onset and development of a first object relation (Green, 1975). The transforming potentiality of "interpretative experiences" rests mainly in the patient's experience of an unsaturated containment—sensorially perceived in a manner akin to the infant's early experiences, and beyond words—that is able to promote psychic change and that rests on Winnicott's (1960) and Bion's (1962) understandings of the deep relational quality of thinking. In particular, interpretative experience" are grounded in (a) the analyst's capacity to create a safe environment (i.e., holding environment), where the setting becomes "more important than interpretation" (Winnicott, 1955-1956, p. 297) for long enough; (b) less frequent transference interpretation in order to leave room for the work of constructing links/bridges between the split mental areas through reverie and other techniques fostering the development of an "unconscious-to-unconscious communication" (Quagelli and Solano, 2016).

Conclusion

Work with unrepresented mental states is becoming increasingly important in contemporary clinical practice where the encounter with non-neurotic patients is more and more frequent. Therefore, it is central for analysts and therapists to further their understandings on these articulated mental functionings in order to develop effective techniques to make contact, receive, transform and give the first representation to these states of mind.

References

Alvarez, A. (1992). *Live Company.* London: Routledge.

Anzieu, D. (1990). Psychic envelopes. London: Karnac.

Aulagnier, P. (1975). *The violence of interpretation.* London: Routledge.

Bergstein, A. (2016). Obsessionality: Modulating the Encounter with Emotional Truth and the Aesthetic Object. *Journal of the American Psychoanalytic Association*, 64(5): 959-982.

Bion, W.R. (1962). A theory of thinking. *International J Psychoanalysis*, 43: 306-310.

Bion, W.R. (1962a). *Learning from experience.* London: Karnac.

Bion, W.R. (1967). Third Seminar – 17 April 1967. In: Aguayo, J., & Malin, B. D. (Eds.). Wilfred Bion: Los Angeles Seminars and Supervision, 2013. London: Karnac.

Bion, W.R. (1970). *Attention and Interpretation.* London: Tavistock Publications.

Bion, W.R. (1977). *The grid and caesura.* London: Karnac.

Bion, W.R. (1979). *A memory of the future: the dawn of oblivion.* London: Karnac.

Bion, W.R. (1992). *Cogitations.* London: Karnac.

Birksted- Breen, D. (2012). Taking time: the tempo of psychoanalysis. *International J Psychoanalysis*, 93: 819-835.

Bleger, J. (1967). Symbiose et ambiguité [*Symbiosis and ambiguity*]. Paris: P.U.F., 1981.

Bronstein, C. (2002). On Free association and psychic reality. *British J Psychotherapy*, 18 (4): 477- 489.

Busch, F.N. (2017). A model for integrating actual neurotic or unrepresented mental states and symbolized aspects of intrapsychic conflicts. *Psychoanalytic Quarterly*, 86(1): 75-108.

Busch, F.N. and Sandberg, L.S. (2014). Unmentalized aspects of panic and anxiety disorders. *Psychodynamic Psychiatry*, 42: 175-195.

Freud, S. (1896). Letter 52 to Wilhelm Fliess (December 6). SE, 1: 233-239.

Freud, S. (1909). *Family Romances*. SE 9: 235-242.

Freud, S. (1913). *On beginning the treatment.* SE 12:121-144.

Green, A. (1975). *On private madness.* London: Karnac.

Green, A. (1983). *The work of the negative.* New York: Free Association Books.

Klein, M. (1926). The psychological principles of early analysis. In *The writings of Melanie Klein* (vol. 1, pp. 128-138). London: Hogarth Press.

Little, M. I. (1985). Winnicott working in areas where psychotic anxieties predominate. *Free Associations*, 1:9-42.

McDougall, J. (1978). Primitive communication and the use of countertransference: Reflections on early psychic trauma and its transference effects. *Contemporary Psychoanalysis*, 14(2):173-209.

Ogden, T. (1997). Reverie and Metaphor: some thoughts on how I work as a psychoanalyst. *International J Psychoanalysis*, 78: 719-732.

O'Shaughnessy, E. (1981). A Commemorative Essay on W.R. Bion's Theory of Thinking. *Journal of Child Psychotherapy*, 7:181-192.

O'Shaughnessy, E. (1982). *Words and working through.* In: Bott Spillius E., Melanie Klein Today, vol. II, pp. 138-151. London: Routledge.

Quagelli, L. and Solano, P. (2016). On Interpretative Experiences: Unconcious-to-Unconcious Communication Through Reverie, Language, and the Setting. *The Psychoanalytic Review*, *103*(2), 169-198.

Rosolato, G. (1985). Eléments de l'interprétation [*Elements of the interpretation*]. Paris: Gallimard.

Roussillon, R. (1991). Paradoxes et situations limites de la psychanalyse [*Paradoxes and limit situation of psychoanalysis*]. PUF: Paris.

Roussillon, R. (1999). Agonie, clivage, symbolization [*Agony, clivage and symbolization*]. Paris: PUF.

Roussillon, R. (2005). La "conversation" psychanalytique: Un divan en latence [*The psychoanalytic "conversation": A couch in latency*]. *Revue Francaise de Psychanalyse*, 69:365-381.

Roussillon, R. (2009). Corps et comportement: langage et messages [*Body and behavior: language and messages*]. *Revue Belgique de Psychanalyse*, 55:23-40.

Roussillon, R. (2011). *Primitive Agony and Symbolization.* London: Karnac.

Roussillon, R. (2012). Theorie du dispositif clinique [*Theory of clinical plan*]. In Manuel de pratique clinique [*Clinical practice manual*] (pp. 97-112). Paris: Payot.

Solano, P. and Quagelli, L. (2015). On "Free Associative Activities". *The Psychoanalytic Review*, 102(2), 237-264.

Stern, D. N. (1985). *The Interpersonal World of the Infant: A View from Psychoanalysis and Developmental Psychology.* New York: Basic Books.

Strachey, J. (1934). The nature of the therapeutic action of psychoanalysis. *International J Psychoanalysis,* 15:127-159.

Winnicott, D. W. (1949) Birth Memories Birth Trauma, Anxiety. In: Winnicott D.W., Collected Papers: Through Paediatrics to Psycho-Analysis, Tavistock, London.

Winnicott, D. W. (1954). Metapsychological and clinical aspects of regression within the psycho-analytical set-up. In *Collected papers: Through paediatrics to psycho- analysis* (pp. 278-294). London: Tavistock, 1958.

Winnicott, D. W. (1955-1956). Clinical varieties of transference. In *Collected papers: Through paediatrics to psycho-analysis* (pp. 295-299). London: Tavistock.

Winnicott, D. W. (1960). The theory of the parent-infant relationship. In: Winnicott D., *The Maturational Processes and the Facilitating Environment.* (pp.37-56). London: Karnac.
Winnicott, D. W. (1971). *Playing and Reality.* London: Routledge.

BIOGRAPHICAL SKETCHES

Paola Solano, MD

Psychiatric Clinic, Department of Neurosciences, Genetics and Maternal Care (DINOG) of the School of Medicine, University of Genova, Italy. She is psychiatrist and psychodynamic psychotherapist working mainly in private practice and completing a PhD study on suicidal behaviors at the Dpt. of Neurosciences of the University of Genova, Italy. Her clinical activity and research focus on the psychoanalytic psychotherapy of psychosis and suicidal behaviors. She is member of the International Association of Suicide Prevention. In the last years, she authored a number of studies concerning psychoanalytic technique in the treatment of psychotic patients published in international psychoanalytic journals and presented in international psychoanalytic conferences. Email address: paola.solano@alice.it.

Luca Quagelli, PhD

Section of “Recherches en Psychanalyse”, VII-Diderot University, Paris, France. He is clinical psychologist and child psychodynamic psychotherapist. He works both in private practice and at the Centre Médico-Psycho-Pédagogique of Courbevoie, Paris. He is completing a research doctorate in the clinic of psychic figurability and the work of the negative at the Section of “Recherches en Psychanalyse”, VII-Diderot University, Paris. His clinical activity and research focus on the psychoanalytic psychotherapy of autistic and psychotic children. In the last years, he authored a number of studies concerning psychoanalytic technique in the treatment of autistic and psychotic children published in international psychoanalytic journals and presented in international psychoanalytic conferences. Email address: lucaquagelli@hotmail.com

In: Psychoanalytic Theory
Editors: K. Martin and M. Siegward
ISBN: 978-1-53612-484-2

Chapter 4

RESISTANCE AND COUNTER-RESISTANCE: A RELATIONAL VIEW

Juhani Ihanus[1*]
Department of Psychology and Logopedics,
University of Helsinki, Finland

ABSTRACT

The article gives first an outline of the concept of resistance in Freudian psychoanalysis. After that, it highlights the vicissitudes of countertransference in psychoanalytic theories from Freudian psychoanalysis to relational, intersubjective and (co-)constructivist psychoanalytic approaches. The author formulates the concept of "counter-resistance", as a special form of countertransference, differentiating its intersubjective aspects. This concept is tied to the integrative, relational and reciprocal psychoanalytic setting and process in which both the analysand and the analyst actively work together through unconscious resistance–counter-resistance dynamics to grasp a better understanding about their situation.

---

[*] Corresponding author address. Email: juhani.ihanus@helsinki.fi.

In this article, the analysis of counter-resistance is proposed to be the supplementary counterpart of the more traditional analysis of resistance. Different forms and variations of counter-resistance of the analyst are presented. The dynamic interplay between resistance of the analysand and counter-resistance of the analyst can be understood as a mainly unconscious arena where the analysand and the analyst collaborate with, and oppose to, each other, touching upon and enacting the developmental roots of their personal emotions, thoughts, motivations, actions, fantasies, conflicts and creative potential.

Counter-resistance can involve certain basic areas that are explicated to include analytic free association, contact, communication, content/material and change. Individually, resistance and counter-resistance can both hinder change and lead to change. The analyst's impatience, vulnerability, assertiveness or outright hostility embedded in unconscious counter-resistance positions can have negative effects on the outcome of analysis. The interference between resistance and counter-resistance can sometimes result in co-resistance phenomena, sabotaging change on both sides. However, there may also be successful working through of co-resistance that paves way toward co-constructive mutual insight and transformation.

This article is not restricted to the psychoanalytic setting, while the resistance–counter-resistance dynamic interaction applies also to the contexts outside the analytic situation. Thus, the author traces a passage from resistance to counter-resistance, via countertransference, in the psychoanalytic process and in the organization and institutionalization of the psychoanalytic theory and discipline.

Keywords: resistance, countertransference, counter-resistance, intersubjectivity, psychoanalytic process, psychoanalytic discipline

INTRODUCTION

When Sigmund Freud (1923) maintained that those who want to call themselves psychoanalysts should accept the "pillars" of psychoanalytic theory that included the unconscious processes, the doctrine of resistance and repression, the infantile sexuality and the Oedipus complex, he did not yet mention transference or countertransference. Countertransference is rarely mentioned in Freud's writings (see for example, Freud, 1910; 1915), and he did not grasp its therapeutic value but saw it as the analyst's unconscious feelings that hindered the analyst to effectively address the patient's problematic areas. The concept of resistance is much more present in Freud's writings.

However, it has taken many decades since Freud's death for more intersubjective or relational conceptions to influence the development of psychoanalysis. The complete psychological works of Sigmund Freud do not contain the term "relation" (*Beziehung*) indexed as a technical psychoanalytic term. In his later writings, Freud was open to the renewal of the basic concepts of psychoanalysis, even admitting that they can be changed in the future, in line with the development of the natural sciences. Especially biology was represented by Freud as a science of the future and as a "land of unlimited possibilities" (Freud, 1920, 20).

In this paper, I reflect on conceptual renewal that has gained from the intersubjective, interpersonal or relational turn in psychoanalysis. The psychoanalytic concept that this paper proposes and expands from Racker's (1958) initial ideas is called "counter-resistance". The traditional concept of resistance was attached in the psychoanalytic setting mainly to the patient while counter-resistance changes the point of view to the analyst's actively configuring effect and to the intersubjective elements of the psychoanalytic process. I will here give a more detailed depiction of this concept that I have previously sketched only shortly (Ihanus, 2015).

First, I will give an outline of the forms and uses of the concept of resistance in Freudian psychoanalysis. After that, I move to highlight the conceptual changes of countertransference from Freudian psychoanalysis to relational and (co-)constructivist psychoanalytic approaches that have led me to differentiate counter-resistance as a special intersubjective aspect of countertransference. This article traces a passage from resistance to counter-resistance, via countertransference, in the psychoanalytic process and in the organization and institutionalization of the psychoanalytic theory and discipline.

RESISTANCE

In their pre-psychoanalytic work, Josef Breuer and Sigmund Freud (1893-1895) already mention "resistance to association" as the single most important form of unconscious resistance. They also analyzed resistance to memorizing. The defensive distortions (omissions) of memory were connected by Freud to repression. Freud (1914) started to talk about "repression resistance" where resistance safeguards repression. When resistance becomes stronger, recollection is more and more replaced by repetitive action. Later, Freud (1926) observed that even if manifestations of conscious resistance were reduced and unconscious ways of repression were made conscious, subtler versions of unconscious resistance continued to influence the patient and demanded the analytic work to move forward to complex transference questions. Already in 1912, Freud had coined the term "transference-resistance" (Freud, 1912a, 106, 108), transference appearing as "the strongest weapon of the resistance" and "the intensity and persistence of the transference" (p. 103) being effected and expressed by resistance. One of Freud's central legacies was to stress the intricate link between resistance and transference – and the protean nature of resistance.

Psychoanalysts have become accustomed to detect and reveal persistent resistance to their field from the side of other disciplinary fields. Psychoanalytic pioneers who started to institutionalize their discipline claimed that their emerging investigative enterprise was surrounded by hostile, reluctant, or indifferent opponents. The opponents were accused of missing the crucial points of psychoanalytic orientation and research. Such argumentation claimed that the opponents misunderstood the basics of psychoanalytic theory and method. They seemed to fail, or refuse to accept the role childhood experiences, unconscious conflicts and motivations and embodied emotional traumas played in personality development. Thus, most of the theories of the social sciences have been labelled by psychoanalysts to contain the seeds of evasion and outright denial of the emotionally and intellectually challenging insights of psychoanalysis. Theories outside the field of psychoanalysis are characterized by psychoanalysts as manifesting a defensive flight from the discoveries of psychoanalysis.

Although there are several orientations in psychology, most of them have made important findings on how the human mind works. Psychoanalysts' task is to openly relate to other kinds of psychological knowledge. It may be that leaning heavily on "depth psychology", psychoanalysis, or psychodynamically oriented psychology has produced dogmatic stances that cannot adapt to changing disciplinary fields. Even if mainstream academic psychology is currently cognitively and neuroscientifically oriented, psychoanalysts who can ease the grip of disciplinary resistance can learn from, and creatively have a dialogue or a polylogue with, different orientations of psychology. No single theory should be prioritized in the interpretations of the human mind and its acts and enactments. An urgent work for psychoanalysts is to be open not only to dissident views but to their own ambivalence, defensiveness and resistances.

Resistance has prevailed on both sides, in "them"/others to psychoanalysts, and in the psychoanalysts themselves ("us") to non-psychoanalytically oriented researchers, theoreticians and psychotherapists, thus making inter- and transdisciplinary dialogues and negotiations difficult. The history of psychoanalysis has plenty of examples of psychoanalytic interpreters who have had their theoretical fixations approaching reductionist "isms", be they Freudian, Jungian, Kleinian, Bionian, or Kohutian. Psychoanalysis has grown several identity shoots, such as relational, intersubjective, interpersonal, communicative, feminist, postcolonial, multicultural, neuropsychoanalytic and integrative. It may be confusing to those who cling to unfaltering theoretical foundations to encounter so many alternative disciplinary and professional identities under the umbrella of psychoanalysis.

Psychoanalysts have recognized that the core of resistance often contains an unconscious conflict between being bound to the past and striving toward new extensions. Several forms of resistance have been analyzed and the becoming conscious of resistance has been used as a tool in psychoanalysis and psychoanalytic psychotherapy. The psychoanalytic process opens unpleasant and distressing possibilities from which people shelter to seemingly more secure hiding places. Insights about growth and development can be painful and are evaded through excuses and self-deceptions. Psychoanalytic thinking and reasoning are not separate from individual and collective emotional conflicts and memories nor from the experiential history of the individual and socio-cultural mind-brain-body.

In the psychoanalytic setting, resistance is directed to free association, communication, contact, content, and, finally, change. Moving away from his earlier drive model, Freud (1926) differentiated ego, id and superego resistances, according to his structural model of the mind. The ego initiated resistances that pertained to repression, transference or gain from illness, id resistance was based on the repetition compulsion, and superego resistance had its source in the feelings of guilt or the need for punishment.

Especially important in the psychoanalytic process are such expressions of resistance that are linked to repression, transference, the feelings of guilt and shame, and the fear of change. In psychoanalytic work, the focus has been on the resistance phenomena of the analysands, though, of course, analysts have their own professional and personal fixations, customs and repetitions that may disturb the analytic process. Only minor attention has been paid to the analysts' own resistance and its ramifications have not been sufficiently delineated.

Freud (1910) made it clear that no psychoanalyst can professionally reach further than his or her own complexes and inner resistances allow. In the same writing, Freud (1910) mentions, for the first time, his concept "countertransference" (*Gegenübertragung*), the analyst's unconscious feelings aroused by the patient, and demands that the practicing analyst should detect and control them. Wilhelm Reich (1933/1972) proposed that "character resistance" manifests itself in the whole personality and concentrates on the exclusion of new and surprising initiatives. Besides more long-term character resistances, there are situational, short-term resistances.

The central role of resistance in psychoanalytic treatment was also in Freud's writings mainly located to the patient. For example, he defined psychoanalytic treatment as "[T]he uncovering and translating of the unconscious" occurring "in the face of a continuous resistance on the part of the patient", while the analyst's work is, not to suggest, but persuade the patient to accept, "by virtue of a better understanding", something that he or she had repressed. Such psychoanalytic treatment was conceived by Freud as an "after-education in overcoming internal resistances" (Freud, 1905, 265-266). The psychoanalyst's character was supposed to be "irreproachable" and he or she should overcome a "mixture of prurience and prudery" (Freud, 1905, 266). On the other hand, an analyst cannot be a model of normalcy and an unfailing educator to reality. An analyst has many changing roles to his or her patient, for example a transference object, a screen for projections, an observer, a sympathizer, a nuisance, an interpreter, but also a model, an educator, a substitute, even a "surgeon". Being such a multirole target will have several effects on the analyst's "character resistance", defences, "cathecting", attachments, self-representations and overall relating.

Developments of the Concept of Countertransference

Freud's ambiguity concerning countertransference is exemplified in his defining it as both resistance/obstacle to analysis (Freud, 1910) and as a therapeutic tool (Freud, 1912a). Freud used the concept only five times in all his published writings. Later developments of the concept of countertransference have been presented in more detail by Stefana (2017) who goes through the changes of the concept influenced by, for example, Melanie Klein and the later British object relations school.

The earliest phase (from about 1909 until 1930) of the concept is characterized by Freudian ideas that held countertransference a hindrance to analytic work, and thus to be inhibited. The second phase (from about 1930 to the late 1940s) was a kind of latent period when the concept of countertransference was defensively objectified in line with positivist ideals derived from the natural sciences insisting on analytic abstinence and neutrality. The third phase (from the late 1940s to the late 1970s) consisted of elaborating and elevating the concept and its instrumental value in the analytic process. The last phase (from the late 1970s onward) has seen a rise of the interpersonal and interactional reconceptualizations of countertransference. (On the phases, see also Körner, 1990; Gysling, 1995.) Here, it suffices to pay attention to only some examples and aspects of the changes of the countertransference concept that concern the increased focus on the intersubjective or interpersonal issues involved in countertransference.

The concept of countertransference has gone through several modifications since Freud's time. Among the pioneers of psychoanalysis, Ferenczi delved most into countertransference issues, becoming a harbinger of the idea that countertransference is not a hindrance to be avoided but a tool for active use, for innovation and interpretation in the analytic process (on Ferenczi and countertransference, see Martín Cabré, 1998; Holmes, 2014). Ferenczi (1919) warned about the pitfall of ''resistance against the countertransference'', the analyst becoming too repellent toward the patient and abruptly closing the analytic work-with-transference. Ferenczi reversed Freud's "surgeon of the soul" and "screen for the projections" metaphors and proceeded toward a maternal conception of countertransference. During analysis, the patient can go through experiential reparations of his/her earlier mother-child relationship.

Like Ferenczi, Winnicott argued that the analyst and the patient constitute an intersubjective relationship, whereby the analyst shows empathy in relation to the analysand's basic needs. Further modifications of this intersubjective conception are Bion's (1962), and later Ogden's (1999), "reverie", Heimann's (1950) "unconscious perceptions of the analyst" and Bollas's (1983) conception of the analyst as a "transforming object" (See Martín Cabré, 1998, 251-252.) In his 1949 paper on hate in countertransference, Winnicott classified countertransference phenomena into three groups: (i) abnormalities in countertransference feelings, relationships and identifications repressed by the analyst; (ii) identifications and tendencies derived from the analyst's personal experiences and development providing a positive setting; (iii) the analyst's "objective countertransference", love and hate reactions to the patient's personality and behavior (Winnicott, 1949, 69). Winnicott (see also Searles's [1979, 191] same kind of idea from his 1949 unpublished article) even set forth that at times and by doses the analyst can express his/her countertransference feelings to the patient – an idea that provoked criticism and that Ferenczi had already expressed within his active technique and later within mutual analysis.

Melanie Klein's pupil Paula Heimann (1950) started to criticize the anonymity of the analyst and the objectifying use of countertransference, stressing the instrumental and constructive value of countertransference. For her, countertransference included "all the feelings which the analyst experiences towards his patient" (Heimann, 1950, 81). It was an essential aspect of the analytic relationship, and "the patient's *creation*", "a part of the patient's personality" (Heimann, 1950, 84). Countertransference is here already seen resulting from an analytic interaction so that the analyst's unconscious understands that of his/her patient. Despite valuing, like Klein, this inter-unconscious (from unconscious-to-unconscious) understanding, Heimann focuses more on conscious and preconscious feelings. The analyst's conscious and preconscious feelings toward the patient began to get more attention in discussions on countertransference. Segal (1977), defending Klein's theory heritage, claimed that countertransference is mainly unconscious, and the analyst can become aware only of its conscious derivatives.

Not all authors on countertransference, in the 1950s and 1960s, were in favor of using countertransference as a therapeutic tool. For example, Annie Reich (1951; 1960; 1965; 1966) argued that countertransference was not useful for communicating with the patient, or for proper interpretation. Reich gave examples of countertransference turned into "acting out", aimed at relieving the analyst's anxiety but leading to failure in the analytic process. Such countertransference as acting out can manifest itself, for example, in the analyst's compulsion to understand, to give compensatory "deep interpretations", to gain "narcissistic gratifications and assurances" or to hand over pedagogic reassurance to the patient (Reich, 1951/1973,

142-145). Reich concluded that the emphasis on countertransference and the analyst's "deep" emotional effect represented an escape from interpretation and a return to "abreaction in the sense it was understood by Ferenczi" (Reich, 1960/1973, 286). She clearly defended ego analysis and the empathic use of one's unconscious for understanding, instead of trying "to work directly with the id and to exert immediate influence upon object relations" (Reich, 1960/1973, 287).

In training analysis with students and in other professional fields as well, Reich detected some intellectual "façades of resistance", theoretical knowledge used for narcissistic purposes, against intuitive and emotional processing (Reich, 1965/1973, 337-338). For Reich, both transference and countertransference contained a pressure to act out, in a positive or negative way. Counter-transference has "innumerable forms" derived from the patient's transference, his/her personality, material or the analytic situation (Reich, 1966/1973, 352-353). Very often the analyst is "stuck" and his/her "blank spots frequently reflect the feeling that the patient mirrors the analyst's unacceptable conflicts" (Reich, 1966/1973, 353-354). Besides transference and countertransference objects, the analytic mirror room is inhabited by real people and not everything that is uttered during analysis belongs to transference-countertransference communication.

The authors of the 1950s and 1960s, like Winnicott, Heimann, A. Reich, Racker, etc. still represented the instrumental view that the analyst's countertransference was receptive and responding and only demonstrated what was happening in the analysand's mind. Not until the late 1970s, a wider interactional and constructive view of countertransference emerged and started to stress the reciprocal intersubjective process where both the analyst and the analysand are in co-operation and active participation, evocating, moving and bridging knowledge and emotions between themselves.

Körner (1990) depicted the intersubjective analytic process that maps the inner conflict, through transference and countertransference, as "unity in contradiction". The analyst and the analysand are both contributing to the relational, at the same time intrapsychic and interpersonal conflict that must be worked through in analytic collaboration. The concept of countertransference is here extended to include "all body sensations, thoughts, feelings and action impulses of the analyst" (Körner, 1990, 97). More extreme representatives of intersubjective conceptions (e.g., Natterson, 1991) have even attempted to replace the concepts of transference and countertransference by the concept of intersubjectivity. (For a detailed critical reader of relational and intersubjective perspectives in psychoanalytic theory and practice, see Mills, 2005.)

Redefining and reconceptualizing of countertransference has continued in various ways. Within the United States, Robert Langs brought forth new theoretical ideas influenced by the British object relations school and communications research. Langs (1978; see also Stefana, 2017, 111-112) maintained that countertransference is an interactional product of the "communicative field" of the analyst and the patient, so that the patient's feelings, phantasies and conscious as well as unconscious communications are partly triggered by the analyst's projective identifications and interventions; Langs was thus suggesting the idea of a patient's countertransference. This interactional view is highly attentive to the bipersonal and bidirectional processes of projective and introjective identification and to the mutual responding between the analyst and the patient.

The relational, intersubjective, interpersonal, communicative and (co-)constructive conceptualizations of countertransference also refer to "enactments", internal "dramas" and "role-relationships" that the analyst and the analysand impose on each other (e.g., Jacobs, 1986; for a history of the term "enactment" in psychoanalysis, see Katz, 2013, chapter 3). For example, Joseph Sandler (1976, 45) proposed that a crucial element in countertransference is the analyst's free-floating "role-responsiveness", the analyst's readiness to see his/her role as a "compromise between his own tendencies or propensities and the role-relationship which the patient is unconsciously seeking to establish" (Sandler, 1976, 47). For Sandler, terms "projection", "externalization", "projective identification" and "putting parts of oneself into the analyst" were not sufficient to approach the processes of the dynamic interrelationship. Instead, Sandler supposed that "a complicated system of unconscious cues, both given and received" is involved not only in transference and countertransference "but in normal object relationships and in the process of temporary or permanent object choice as well" (Sandler, 1976, 47).

Further elaborating Winnicott's, Bion's and André Green's (1975; 2004) ideas, Thomas Ogden (1994) introduced the concept of "the intersubjective analytic third" or "the analytic third". As an unconscious intersubjective co-creation by the analyst and the analysand, the analytic third at the same time creates the analyst and the analysand. From this point of view, the "matrix" (Ogden 1991) of transference-countertransference does not create similar but dynamically dialectic and mutual modes of experience. For Ogden, "the simultaneity of the dialectic of oneness and twoness, of individual subjectivity and intersubjectivity" is "the foundation of the psychoanalytic relationship" (1994, 8) and informs the changing field of experience concerning transference and countertransference. Boesky (1990) has emphasized the uniqueness of each transference-countertransference interaction.

What Bion (1959) called "attacks on linking" included the patient's breaking links to his/her own mental functions and to the relations between his/her own mind and that of the analyst – who was supposed to approach the patient in every analytic session without preconceived and distorting ideas, without memory, desire or understanding (Bion, 1967; see also Casement, 1990). Envious, destructive and self-defeating attacks on linking can also be directed to the relation between the analyst and the validity of his/her interpretation, and to the relation between the patient's present self-understanding and his potential, expanding future self-understanding. Like Bion before him, Ogden thought that such attacks on linking could be approached through the reveries in the analytic process.

COUNTER-RESISTANCE

Concerning the analysand's resistances, the analyst has special countertransference versions (mostly unconscious feelings, thoughts, fantasies and attitudes) that focus on resisting the analysand's resistances. I propose such countertransference relating to be called "counter-resistance". It can sometimes intensify to regressive states, like impatience, boredom, love/hate reactions, manipulation, indoctrination or overeager forcing change for which the patient should be given more time. In such states, the analyst's counter-resistance can be an obstacle to the patient's becoming able to immerse him-/herself in working through and overcoming resistance. The culmination of resistance should be allowed to proceed in the atmosphere of non-intrusive co-operation.

Freud (1914) pointed out that this process is trying to both the patient and the analyst. Nevertheless, it should be given time because the working through and overcoming of resistance makes possible the biggest changes in the patient (Freud, 1914). Even in this context, Freud does not speak anything about the possible change in the analyst's mind because of the collaborative working through and overcoming of the analyst's own resistances.

Racker is probably the only author who has previously referred to "counter-resistance". His position was still more instrumental than intersubjective, detaching the analyst from the patient. He thought that counter-resistances "indicate (as do the patient's resistances against communicating certain thoughts) the most important conflicts within the patient" and are "the expression of the analyst's identification with the patient's resistances, even though they may at the same time be related to a conflict within the analyst" (Racker, 1958, 221). Counter-resistance may result in deterring or giving too fast interpretations because of a confused understanding of the patient's personality. Racker (1957, 326) has also differentiated the patient's transference resistance and the analyst's countertransference resistance, while Gittelson (1952) made a difference between the "analyst's transferences" (reactions to the patient as a whole) and the "analyst's countertransferences" (reactions to the partial aspects of the patient).

The resistance-counter-resistance dynamic interaction applies also to the contexts outside the analytic situation, to the organization and institutionalization of psychoanalysis. In the history of psychoanalysis, resistance has been mostly located outside the psychoanalytic "us group".

Becoming conscious of and working through one's inner, and "in-group" resistance is tedious and demands patience, but it can lead to positive change in the psychoanalytic profession.

When resistance appears, at the same time it contains plenty of meaningful, humanly touching, and valuable experience that cannot be forced or precipitated. Meanings as such do not create conflict but the "cathectic emphases" (Ikonen & Rechardt, 2010, 73) attached to meanings and meaning negotiations do create conflict. If the exclusive attitude ("That is not our business/practice") is dominant, there is hardly any breathing space for inter- and transdisciplinary initiative, or for cross-fertilization. Psychoanalysts can develop their skills for studying and clarifying the various motivational bases of resistance: social, cultural, political and historical rituals, and individual routines, manners and repetitions. What makes us maintain resistance, the avoidance of the unknown? Does it ease one's living, or suck one's resources that would be needed for realizing one's potential?

Psychoanalysts have transferences to their research data (people, events, settings, etc.) What psychoanalysts call countertransference, the unconscious emotions of the analyst in relation to the analysand's thoughts, emotions, and behavior, is also present in the psychoanalysts' relations to the representatives of other disciplines, and their interpretations. Psychoanalysts' countertransference can fuse with regressive states that imply, for example, impatience, unbelief, arrogance, and manipulative maneuvers that are directed against resistances to psychoanalysis, from other fields of knowledge. These states can also be called psychoanalysts' "counter-resistances" that may sabotage collaborative efforts and new insights and become self-defeating. Psychoanalysts' counter-resistance to other disciplines can be a source of regression or progression.

Personality features, attachment styles, and defences of psychoanalysts can be inflexible: here I stand and cannot do otherwise. Unconscious and only partly conscious counter-resistances of psychoanalysts can hinder interdisciplinary contacts, but they can also block new ideas that originate from those who are seen to be stubborn opponents of psychoanalysis.

Perhaps it is easier to become aware of others' resistance phenomena than of one's own counter-resistances that hide obsessive ideas, fixed principles and preferences, and the ritualized devaluations of other routes to knowledge. Epistemological inflexibility can include opposition to emerging dissident theories that are considered irritating and adding too many painful challenges. Adopted "right doctrines" are thus defended against "false notions".

The specialties of psychoanalytic knowledge construction do not justify isolation from scientific community and its critical, often provocative debates. The psychoanalytic "us group" may have adopted fantasies and representations of exceptionalism. Psychoanalysis has certainly met simplified, distorted, and hostile receptions in scientific discussion. Psychoanalytic approaches evoke both intellectual and emotional involvement and may thus lead to resistance and outright maliciousness that help the critics of psychoanalysis to camouflage their fears of their own unconscious conflicts.

Psychoanalytic or any other knowledge does not get constructed only so that I know, or that we know what is permanently right. Observing and knowing one's self otherwise – taking one's chances – gives a changing ground to the personal and professional development of psychoanalysts. Mutual efforts at creating new connections and horizons for understanding complex and dynamic phenomena are needed both in research and in psychoanalytic practice. The "theoretical identities" of psychoanalysts reflect their personal proclivities, attitudes, and values. In psychotherapy research, psychodynamically oriented psychotherapists have usually scored higher than (cognitive-)behavior therapists in intuition, openness for experience, need for cognition, risk-taking, and ambiguity tolerance. Whether this applies to the theoretical orientations of psychoanalysts as well, has not yet been studied. There are also biases in scientific research connected with using too much intuition, and tolerating ambiguity and unfounded assumptions.

Contradictions between different approaches can be a guarantee of lively scientific discussion. On the other hand, progress in research is often enhanced by multiple approaches and voices. Dialogical and polyphonic psychoanalysis is part of the human sciences that may have fruitful contacts with several scientific fields, opening resistance, and heading toward updated insights in self-observation, self-knowledge, and self-realization.

In his pilot study, "In the mind of the teacher", reported at the XVIII International Forum of Psychoanalysis in Kaunas (September 17, 2014), Miguel Angel Gonzalez-Torres compared psychoanalytic journals with psychiatric, general medicine and theoretical physics journals, noting down the number of bibliographical references and the number of recent references (published within the last ten years). The percentages of recent references were in psychoanalytic journals only around 20%, while in psychiatric and theoretical physics journals it was around 50, and in the field of general medicine 80. Such results raise a disturbing doubt that psychoanalytic knowledge is heavily dependent on old authorities, avoiding confrontations with their views. We can ask whether psychoanalysis at large has the same kind of situation as American psychoanalysis, more "a multiplicity of authoritarian orthodoxies (…) rather than a scientific discourse," as depicted by Arnold M. Cooper (2008, 235).

It is not the repetition of old errors but openness to rethinking that characterizes scientific advancement, also within psychoanalysis. Psychoanalysis is not a closed knowledge system but an unfinished enterprise, ready for self-evaluation and change. Its radical reformism and awakening of consciousness are based on re-appraising personal, social and cultural issues that were formerly considered self-evident. Surely, psychoanalysts do not resist observing and reanalyzing their own assumptions and conceptions, do they?

When the analyst's countertransference reactions oppose the patient's resistance to contact and change, the ensuing phenomena such as exclusion, forgetfulness, boredom, frustration, and repulsion attest to "counter-resistance". In such situations, the analyst may displace responsibility from him-/herself and claim the patient to be responsible for the errors and even the shortcomings of his/her analytic practice and method. The analyst then refuses to analyze his/her professional attitude and skills, and places him-/herself to an external judgmental position, not to an internal and interactive relationship (cf. Raabe, 2005, 511-512). Avoiding the criticism of one's approach and method does not prepare a fertile ground for self-reflection and -transformation. In his recommendations to physicians practicing psychoanalysis, Freud (1912b, 116) reminded them of the "temptation of projecting outwards some of the peculiarities of his [the analyst's] own personality (…) into the field of science, as a theory having universal validity". For example, psychoanalytic case histories tend to pay less attention to impasses, errors, and fumbling than to successful choices and interpretations from the side of the analyst.

In their psychoanalytic work, psychoanalysts have mostly become accustomed to detecting and recognizing the resistance phenomena of the analysands that show conflicts between sticking to the past and reaching toward the future. Numerous forms of resistance have been differentiated, and the aim has been to make the analysands become conscious of their individual ways of resistance, so that favourable changes could be realized. The psychoanalytic process often opens unpleasant, pressing and painful possibilities that are warded off by seeking an apparently more secure refuge, and, through different pretexts, by evading their testing. Our thinking and reasoning are not separate from ambivalence and memories; likewise, our somatically manifested resistance phenomena are not without their links to the experiential history of our mind.

Where resistance manifests itself, there are also several personal meanings hidden – and gradually emerging to be approached and worked through. Psychoanalysis can proceed tactfully, with and beside resistance, by observing it and plumbing its developmental and motivational roots. Repetitions, rituals, manners and routines can also facilitate people's lives. However, abundantly used they tend to schematize and stiffen the familiar and ordinary, to exclude the uncanny and the unknown, and to dismiss experiential qualities that are strange to oneself. To keep up resistances, one must spend resources that would otherwise support personal growth and self-realization.

Since Freud, the psychoanalytic profession has stressed the patient's transforming of the unconscious into the conscious by recognizing and working through of resistance. With the help of automatized regulation of displeasure, an individual is prone to persistently repress the unconscious, protect oneself from the dangerous perceptions and perspectives of change. At the same time, a person is about to become marginalized from his or her life, an outsider to him- or herself. Although the working through of resistance is cumbersome and demands patience, Freud (1914) thought that it will finally change the patient most and show the assets of psychoanalysis compared with the suggestive and manipulative modes of treatment.

In this article, I propose the relational analysis of counter-resistance to be the supplementary counterpart of the more traditional analysis of resistance. The unconscious and partly preconscious and conscious counter-resistance phenomena in the psychoanalytic setting can be harmful "attacks on linking" and change (negative counter-resistance), but they can also be in the service of, of for, change (positive counter-resistance). While resisting the patient's resistance, the analyst can postpone or even foreclose the patient's possibilities for insight. The analyst's impatience, vulnerability, assertiveness or outright hostility embedded in unconscious counter-resistance positions can have negative effects on the outcome of analysis.

The interference between resistance and counter-resistance can sometimes result in "co-resistance" phenomena, sabotaging change on both sides. However, there may also be successful working through of co-resistance that paves way toward co-constructive mutual insight and transformation. The dynamic interplay between resistance of the analysand and counter-resistance of the analyst can be understood as a mainly unconscious arena where the analysand and the analyst collaborate with, and oppose to, each other, touching upon and enacting the developmental roots of their personal emotions, thoughts, fantasies, scenes, conflicts and creative potential.

The analyst's inflexible partly unconscious and partly preconscious and conscious counter-resistance feelings, thoughts and attitudes in the analytic setting may be related to free association (e.g., "follow the rule of psychoanalysis"), communication (e.g., "impossible to say nothing about that"), contact ("this cannot be so tedious"), content/material ("not that same stuff again") and change ("please, change, I cannot stand this procrastination"). It may be a more frequent version of counter-resistance to try to hasten change, but another version is to slow down change ("not that kind of change, do not go in that direction"). Then the analyst is not able to separate from the patient, to terminate analysis in proper time (even if analysis is, in a way, "interminable"), and to allow the patient's further development, becoming independent of the analyst whom the patient will in the end leave alone.

Non-creative, mechanical or fixed forms of binding (not letting the false constructions go for a change to come) can increase malignant resistance and counter-resistance, while more movable, mobile, maneuverable and transformative forms of binding may assist playful, autonomous, emancipating and creative processes in and outside the analytic situation. (On the forms of binding, cf. Ikonen & Rechardt, 2010, 65-70.) Finally, through its positive versions, counter-resistance can open doors to co-operation, co-emergence, even to co-interpretation that is not a stabile construct resisting the transformative and mutual play of memory, desire and understanding.

The analytic skill of listening between the lines, gaps and silences demands openness to the possible pitfall that me and my practice can neglect change-in-interaction, my master interpretation resisting contradiction and cross-interpretation that would contribute to meaningful moment-to-moment co-emerging and co-fading for new polyphonic and multilocational constellations to appear. It is hard to admit, and reflect on, the effects of stubborn positioning ("I, the analyst, must not be countered nor interpreted") on the analytic stalemate where too secure interpretations avoid something unsettling and do not start a movement-in-interaction for joint exploration of what we do not understand.

Bracha L. Ettinger (2009, 113-114) redefines resistance in matrixial and virtual worlds: "In a mysterious way, the subject keeps emerging, assuming its own resistance to the outside and to the inside. Since the

I functions by borderlinking and borderspacing, its affective and effective zone is in constant negotiation, on an in-between level which is neither that of the collective nor that of the individual nor that of inter-relations. And yet, the subject persists and must confront its own narcissism and paranoia, again and again."

Further, Ettinger (2009, 121-122) repositions resistance by suggesting: "Resistance is not a passive aggressive sulking. It is not attack, guilt, shame, regret. (…) resistance is a working for, not against, a re-working for trust, again and again. Virtu(re)al openness depends on this re-working, re-trusting, re-specting. Resistance reaches an ethical level when compassion becomes a perspective – a value. (…) Resistance is not terrorism. Indifference kills resistance, hate kills resistance." Sharing, "wit(h)nessing", recreates resistance for "communicaring" and produces "unexpected, surprising transgressive assembling of I and non-I" (2009, 122). The defensive, objectifying and instrumental use of empathy ("without com-passion"), transference (without transjects), countertransference (without relating), resistance and counter-resistance (without sharing), and interpretation (without cross-interpretation) signifies an empty analytic space, a lifeless *Stilleben* (without movable, moving and touching interaction).

When relying on resistance and counter-resistance that are working for, not against, trust and mutual in-specting and re-specting, psychoanalysis can allow its hard-to-digest germs to grow and develop through searching narratives and enactments that spin meaningful experiential weaves. Such psychoanalysis is not stuck in stagnant rituals (see Hoffman, 1998) of resistance and counter-resistance but its freely floating responsiveness accepts both spontaneous expressions and reflective approaches. The enactments of resistance and counter-resistance on the analytic performance scene can be creative and lively encounter-events with joint creations, scripts, dialogues and non-verbal expressions – gestures and postures without posing.

Basic psychoanalytic concepts and theories, as intellectual abstractions and idealizations, hide and cover complex unconscious mutual evocations and responses and unique interrelationships, delivering the rational orders of knowledge about infinite sets and spaces. Concepts like transference, countertransference, resistance and counter-resistance are unfinished, to be further negotiated, empathically cathected, contradicted and experientially tried in the on-going workshop of psychoanalysis, together with other "schools" and disciplines. Freud (1923) had already acknowledged that psychoanalysis is always unfinished and ready to revise or change its doctrines. Like physics and chemistry, psychoanalysis admits that its basic concepts are imprecise and its conditions temporary, to be elaborated.

There is no such (isolated) thing as an analyst or an analysand. Perhaps, to "reinvent" the intersubjects of the analyst and the analysand, we need to be ready to reattune the analytic scene and the characters so that they are not at the mercy of relentless resistances and counter-resistances but resonate with and within interactive practices and dialogues. The "fallacy of understanding" (Levenson, 1972) is constantly lurking behind and in psychoanalytic practice, theory and institutions. The choreography of the interplay in the living theater of psychoanalysis is at its best a mobile of surprises, not resisting transformation.

REFERENCES

Bion, W. R. (1959). Attacks on linking. *International Journal of Psychoanalysis, 40* (5-6), 308-315.

Bion, W. R. (1962). *Learning from experience.* London: William Heinemann.

Boesky, D. (1990). The psychoanalytic process and its components. *Psychoanalytic Quarterly 59* (4), 550-584.

Bollas, C. (1983). Expressive uses of the countertransference. *Contemporary Psychoanalysis, 19* (1), 1-34.

Breuer, J. & Freud, S. (1893-1895). Studies on hysteria. *The Standard Edition of the Complete Psychological Works of Sigmund Freud* (= *S. E.*), *II*. London: The Hogarth Press.

Casement, P. (1990). *Further learning from the patient: The analytic space and process*. London: Routledge.

Cooper, A. M. (2008). American psychoanalysis today: A plurality of orthodoxies. *Journal of the American Academy of Psychoanalysis and Dynamic Psychiatry*, *36* (2), 235-253.

Ettinger, B. L. (2009). Fragilization and resistance. In B. L. Ettinger, *Fragilization and resistance* (pp. 97-134). Helsinki: Aivojen yhteistyön muistivihkot.

Ferenczi, S. (1919/1980). Technical difficulties in the analysis of a case of hysteria. In S. Ferenczi, *Further contributions to the theory and technique of psycho-analysis* (pp. 189-197). New York: Brunner / Mazel.

Freud, S. (1905 [1904]). On psychotherapy. *S. E.*, *VII*, 255-268.

Freud, S. (1910). The future prospects of psycho-analytic therapy. *S. E.*, *XI*, 139-151.

Freud, S. (1912a). The dynamics of transference. *S. E.*, *XII*, 97-108.

Freud, S. (1912b). Recommendations to physicians practising psycho-analysis. *S. E.*, *XII*, 109-120.

Freud, S. (1914). Remembering, repeating and working-through. *S. E.*, *XII*, 147-156.

Freud, S. (1920). *Beyond the pleasure principle*. *S. E.*, *XVIII*, 1-64.

Freud, S. (1923). "Psycho-analysis" and "The libido theory". *S. E.*, *XVIII*, 235-259.

Freud, S. (1926). *Inhibitions, symptoms and anxiety*. *S. E.*, *XX*, 87-174.

Gittelson, M. (1952). The emotional position of the analyst in the psychoanalytic situation. *International Journal of Psychoanalysis, 33* (1), 1-10.

Green, A. (1975). The analyst, symbolization and absence in the analytic setting (On changes in analytic practice and analytic experience) – In memory of D. W. Winnicott. *International Journal of Psychoanalysis, 56* (1), 1-22.

Green, A. (2004). Thirdness and psychoanalytic concepts. *Psychoanalytic Quarterly, 73* (1), 99-135.

Gysling, A. (1995). *Die analytische Antwort: Eine Geschichte der Gegenübertragung in Form von Autorenportraits*. Tübingen: edition diskord. [The analytic answer: A history of countertransference in the form of author portraits.]

Heimann, P. (1950). On counter-transference. *International Journal of Psychoanalysis, 31* (1), 81-84.

Hoffman, I. Z. (1998). *Ritual and spontaneity in the psychoanalytic process: A dialectical-constructivist view*. Hillsdale: The Analytic Press.

Holmes, J. (2014). Countertransference before Heimann: An historical exploration. *Journal of the American Psychoanalytic Association, 62* (4), 603-629.

Ihanus, J. (2015). Resistances and counter-resistances in psychohistory. *Clio's Psyche, 22* (3), 209-213.

Ikonen, P. & Rechardt, E. (2010). *Thanatos, shame, and other essays: On the psychology of destructiveness*. London: Karnac Books

Jacobs, T. (1986). On countertransference enactments. *Journal of the American Psychoanalytic Association, 34* (2), 289-307.

Katz, G. (2013). *The play within the play: The enacted dimension of psychoanalytic process*. London: Routledge.

Körner, J. (1990). Übertragung und Gegenübertragung, eine Einheit im Widerspruch. *Forum der Psychoanalyse, 6* (2), 87-104. [Transference and countertransference, unity in contradiction.]

Langs, R. J. (1978). *The listening process*. New York: Jason Aronson.

Levenson, E. A. (1972). *The fallacy of understanding: An inquiry into the changing structure of psychoanalysis*. New York: Basic Books.

Martín Cabré, L. J. (1998). Ferenczi's contribution to the concept of countertransference. *International Forum of Psychoanalysis, 7* (4), 247-255.

Mills, J. (ed.) (2005). *Relational and intersubjective perspectives in psychoanalysis: A critique*. Lanham, MD: Jason Aronson.

Natterson, J. (1991). *Beyond countertransference: The therapist's subjectivity in the therapeutic process*. Northvale, NJ: Jason Aronson.

Ogden, T. H. (1991). Analysing the matrix of transference. *International Journal of Psychoanalysis, 72* (4), 593-605.

Ogden, T. H. (1994). The analytic third: Working with intersubjective clinical facts. *International Journal of Psychoanalysis, 75* (1), 3-19.

Ogden, T. H. (1999). *Reverie and interpretation: Sensing something human*. Northvale, NJ: Jason Aronson.

Raabe, P. B. (2005). Reinterpreting psychiatric diagnoses. *Janus Head, 8* (2), 509-521.

Racker, H. (1957). The meanings and uses of countertransference. *Psychoanalytic Quarterly, 26* (3), 303-357.

Racker, H. (1958). Counterresistance and interpretation. *Journal of the American Psychoanalytic Association, 6* (2), 215-221.

Reich, A. (1951/1973). On countertransference. In A. Reich, *Psychoanalytic contributions* (pp. 136-154). New York: International Universities Press.

Reich, A. (1960/1973). Further remarks on countertransference. In A. Reich, *Psychoanalytic contributions* (pp. 271-287).

Reich, A. (1965/1973). Special types of resistance in traininganalysis. In A. Reich, *Psychoanalytic contributions* (pp. 334 343).

Reich, A. (1966/1973). Empathy and countertransference. In A. Reich, *Psychoanalytic contributions* (pp. 344-360).

Reich, W. (1933/1972). *Character analysis*. New York: Farrar, Straus and Giroux.

Sandler, J. (1976). Countertransference and role-responsiveness. *International Review of Psychoanalysis, 3* (1), 43-47.

Searles, H. (1979). *Countertransference and related subjects: Selected papers*. New York: International Universities Press.

Segal, H. (1977). Countertransference. *International Journal of Psychoanalytic Psychotherapy, 6* (1), 31-37.

Stefana, A. (2017). *History of countertransference: From Freud to the British Object Relations School*. London and New York: Routledge.

Winnicott, D. W. (1949). Hate in the counter-transference. *International Journal of Psychoanalysis, 30* (1), 69-74.

INDEX

D

E

J

K

L

M

Q

R

S

V

W